LONDON'S RAILWAYS
1967-1977

LONDON'S RAILWAYS 1967-1977

A SNAP SHOT IN TIME

JIM BLAKE

Published in 2015 by
Pen & Sword Transport
an imprint of
Pen & Sword Books Ltd
47 Church Street
Barnsley
South Yorkshire
S70 2AS

ISBN 978 1 47383 384 5

Typeset by Nigel Pell
Printed and bound by Replika Press Pvt. Ltd.

Pen & Sword Books Ltd incorporates the imprints of Pen & Sword
Archaeology, Atlas, Aviation, Battleground, Discovery, Family
History, History, Maritime, Military, Naval, Politics, Railways, Select,
Transport, True Crime, and Fiction, Frontline Books, Leo Cooper,
Praetorian Press, Seaforth Publishing and Wharncliffe.

For a complete list of Pen & Sword titles please contact
PEN & SWORD BOOKS LIMITED
47 Church Street, Barnsley, South Yorkshire, S70 2AS, England
E-mail: enquiries@pen-and-sword.co.uk
Website: www.pen-and-sword.co.uk

CONTENTS

ABOUT THE AUTHOR

JIM BLAKE was born at the end of 1947, just five days before the 'Big Four' railway companies, and many bus companies – including London Transport – were nationalised by the Labour government under Clement Attlee.

Like most young lads born in the early post-war years, he soon developed a passionate interest in railways, the myriad steam engines still running on Britain's railways in those days in particular. The busy North London Line on which locomotives of both LMS and LNER origin could be seen was just five minutes walk away from his home, and he can still remember being taken to a bomb site overlooking Canonbury Junction in his pushchair to see them.

However, because his home in Canonbury Avenue, Islington was also just a few minutes walk from North London's last two tram routes, the 33 in Essex Road and the 35 in Holloway Road and Upper Street, which ran through the famous Kingsway tram subway to reach Victoria Embankment and south London, Jim developed an equal interest in buses and trolleybuses to that in railways, and has retained both until the present day. In addition, Jim's home was in the heart of North London's trolleybus system, with route 611 actually passing his home, and one of the busiest and complicated trolleybus junctions in the world at The Nag's Head, Holloway, a short ride away along Holloway Road. Here, the overhead wires almost blotted out the sky!

Jim was educated at his local Highbury County Grammar School, and later at Kingsway College, by coincidence a stone's throw from the old tram subway. He was first bought a camera for his fourteenth birthday at the end of 1961, which was immediately put to good use photographing the last London trolleybuses in North West London on their very snowy last day a week later. Three years later, he started work as an administrator for the old London County Council at County Hall, just across the road from Waterloo Station, where in the summer of 1967, the last steam engines hauling passenger trains in the south of England would run.

By now, Jim's interest in buses and trolleybuses had expanded to include those of other operators, and he travelled throughout England and Wales between 1961 and 1968 in pursuit of them, being able to afford to travel further afield after starting work! These journeys tied in perfectly with visiting engine sheds up and down the country, particularly in the northwest England where the last steam engines would run in 1968. He also bought a colour ciné-camera in 1965, with which he was able to capture what is now very rare footage of long-lost buses, trolleybuses and steam locomotives. Where the latter are concerned, he was one of the initial purchasers of the unique British Railways Standard class 8, No 71000 *Duke of Gloucester*, which was the last ever passenger express locomotive built for use in Britain. Other preservationists laughed at the group which purchased what in effect was a cannibalised hulk from Barry scrapyard at the end of 1973, but they laughed on the other side of their faces when, after extensive and innovative rebuilding, it steamed again in 1986. It has since become one of the best-known and loved preserved British locomotives, often returning to the main lines.

Following the demise of British Railways steam engines in 1968, Jim began to take a more specific interest in London's Underground railway. In particular, the short and isolated Northern City Line, which literally ran beneath his original home on its way from Finsbury Park to Moorgate but which should have been greatly extended to cover the London & North Eastern Railway's branches from Finsbury Park to Highgate, Alexandra Palace, East Finchley, High Barnet, Mill Hill and Edgware, became a 'pet theme'. Work on this extension had to be put in abeyance during Second World War, and despite much work having been completed on it, the scheme was abandoned in the early 1950s and as much as £3,000,000 (at 1939 values) of public money thereby wasted. With co-author Jonathan James, Jim published the first definitive book on this scandalous waste, *Northern Wastes*, in 1987 and that book has subsequently gone through three reprints.

Although Jim spent thirty-five years in local government administration, with the LCC's successor, the Greater London Council, then Haringey Council and finally literally back on his old doorstep, with Islington Council, Jim also took a break from office drudgery in 1974/75 and actually worked on the buses as a conductor at London Transport's Clapton Garage, on local routes 22, 38 and 253. Working on the latter, a former tram and trolleybus route, in particular was an unforgettable experience! He was recommended for promotion as an inspector, but rightly thought that taking such a job with the surname Blake was unwise in view of the then-current character of the same name and occupation in the *On the Buses* TV series and

films, and so declined the offer and returned to County Hall!

By this time, Jim had begun to have his transport photographs published in various books and magazines featuring buses and railways, and also started off the North London Transport Society, which catered for enthusiasts interested in both subjects. In conjunction with this group, he has also compiled and published a number of books on these subjects since 1977, featuring many of the 100,000 or so transport photographs he has taken over the years.

Also through the North London Transport Society, Jim became involved in setting up and organising various events for transport enthusiasts in 1980, notably the North Weald Bus Rally which the group took over in 1984, and has raised thousands of pounds for charity ever since. These events are still going strong today.

In addition to his interest in public transport, Jim also has an interest in the popular music of the late 1950s and early 1960s, in particular that of the eccentric independent record producer, songwriter and manager Joe Meek, in whose tiny studio above a shop in Holloway Road (not far from the famous trolleybus junction) he wrote and produced *Telstar* by The Tornados, which became the first British pop record to make No1 in America, at the end of 1962, long before The Beatles had even been heard of over there! When Joe died in February 1967, Jim set up an appreciation society for his music, which has a very distinctive sound. That society is also still going strong today, too.

Jim also enjoys a pint or two (and usually more) of real ale, and has two grown-up daughters and three grandchildren at the time of writing. He still lives in North London, having moved to his present home in Palmers Green in 1982.

INTRODUCTION

This collection of photographs dates from the period 1967 to 1977, a time when London's railways were undergoing a great upheaval. Not only did this period see the final withdrawal of steam traction from both British Railways and London Transport use, it also saw the demise of many of the early diesel and electric locomotives and multiple units on both systems. At the time the earliest of these pictures were taken, the latter did not have much of a following amongst serious railway enthusiasts – including myself – but some forty to fifty years later, many early British Railways diesels which have survived into preservation are now just as popular on Britain's heritage railways as steam locomotives. Unfortunately, the same cannot be said of most of the early British Railways electric rolling stock and most of that of London Transport origin, due to the obvious operational limitations – particularly with the fourth-rail method of current collection used on the Underground.

My own interest in London's railways is typical of that of a youngster born in the early post-war years: in fact I was actually born just five days before British Railways took over the 'Big Four' main line companies on 1 January 1948! In those days, most young lads were 'trainspotters' and I was no exception, especially as I was brought up in Canonbury, near to the busy North London Line and also with such places as Finsbury Park, Kings Cross, St. Pancras and Euston stations a short bus (or trolleybus!) ride away. Because we had North London's last

trams on our doorstep, as well as the largest trolleybus network in the world in the area, I gained an equal interest in London Transport's bus, coach, tram, trolleybus and underground operations. We had, in fact, the latter's stunted Northern City branch running directly beneath our home in Canonbury Avenue!

Unfortunately, by the time my 'spotting' interest had developed into the more serious one of transport photography, most steam engines working in the London area had been replaced by diesel or electric traction – with the notable exception of the former London & South Western main line of the Southern Region out of Waterloo. By chance, when I left school at the end of 1964, my first job was as a technical clerk for the chief engineer's department of the London County Council at County Hall – just across the road from Waterloo Station. So at least I was able to record on both still and ciné-film steam operation on that last London main line until its final demise in July 1967.

By this time, my interest in buses and trolleybuses had taken precedence over that in railways, photographically speaking, and other than making several treks up to the northwest for the last British Railways steam engines of all, did little railway-wise. Indeed, as it was also for various friends of mine brought up on steam, it was virtually taboo for me to photograph diesels or electrics, other than the latter on the Underground!

However, that began to change as early BR diesel and electric types began to be replaced as the 1960s drew to a close. In particular, the pre-war Southern electric units which I saw most work-days at Waterloo became more interesting to me.

Aside from locomotives and rolling stock, I have always had an interest in railway architecture, particularly stations. There were still a good few disused stations in my local area, notably on the former Great Northern branches from Finsbury Park to Highgate and Alexandra Palace which should have become part of London Transport's Northern Line in 1940. The story of that uncompleted project has always been close to my heart, and indeed I published the first definitive book on the subject, *Northern Wastes*, in the 1980s. Therefore the photographs in this book also include some of interesting and disused stations as they were in the late 1960s and 1970s, along

with a few illustrating the wasted works on this uncompleted Underground extension as it was then.

I have arranged the photographs in this book in a series of 'themes', rather than in chronological order. Although much of the material included relates to British Railways and LT Underground lines in my local North London area, not all of it does and therefore I hope readers will find this to be a reasonable coverage of railways in and around London. I have, generally, taken the former London Transport area as the limit of geographical coverage.

My thanks go to Colin Clarke and John Scott-Morgan for their help in putting this book together.

Jim Blake

9 November 2014

On 6th June 1971, a brand new train of C69 Stock passes West Hampstead station with a special bound for an open day at Neasden Depot marking the passing of steam trains on the Underground. These units replaced CO/CP stock on the Circle and Hammersmith & City Lines, and remained in service until the spring of 2014.

GREAT NORTHERN SUBURBAN

The Great Northern suburban lines, running from Kings Cross, Broad Street and Moorgate (City widened lines) are those, on the former British Railways network, that I have always known best. Not only have I always lived locally to them, but I also have fond memories of seeing sturdy little Gresley N2 class 0-6-2Ts hauling their rakes of quad- or quint-art carriages through Canonbury Junction (where as a very small child I can remember being taken in my pushchair to a bomb-site to watch them) or at Kings Cross and Finsbury Park – including on the ill-fated shuttle service from the latter to Alexandra Palace, withdrawn in July 1954. Also, an aunt and her family who had lived in Highbury Hill moved out to Stevenage New Town in 1956, and we often visited them at the very time when steam was giving way to diesel traction: more's the pity I was too young then to have been able to photograph the changing

scene! I even commuted in the end on these lines, from Palmers Green to Highbury & Islington, between January 1989 and my retirement at the end of 2000, from my last job as a senior administrator at Islington Council. Ironically, the Class 313 electric units introduced to these services in 1976, when the link to the former Northern City Underground line from Finsbury Park to Drayton Park originally built for tube trains running to Highgate and Alexandra Palace in 1939 was finally brought into use, and which I travelled on, are still in use as this book is put together in the summer of 2014. They are now the oldest passenger rolling stock in regular commuter use on the entire national rail network – except for the 1938 stock former tube trains on the Isle of Wight, which are the same type the Class 313 units replaced on the former Northern City Line between Drayton Park and Moorgate when they were new.

Typical of Great Northern suburban services in the period this book covers prior to electrification, Brush 2 diesel No.5626 has arrived at Welwyn Garden City with a down stopping service in the summer of 1973. The splendid Great Northern signal box seen here will also be swept away when electrification of these services takes place some three years later.

On 13 October 1972, English Electric Type 4 diesel, No 278 departs from the original Stevenage station with the down *Cambridge Buffet Express*. This station was situated to the extreme north of Stevenage 'old town', which itself was north of the huge new town established a few years after the war, part of which was in fact closer as the 'crow flies' to Knebworth station. But a new station to serve the New Town centre, which was directly beside the main line just north of Langley Junction, did not figure in the development plans for the new town and would not materialise until 1973! I well remember how the old station buildings here would rattle as express trains thundered through, particularly when hauled by an A4 Pacific or a Deltic diesel. Also of note in this view is the BR-style totem sign still in use, along with gas lamps; a new road bridge has been built just north of the original one, which will be demolished upon electrification.

RIGHT: Seen from the 'spotters' observation platform' erected by the London County Council in Finsbury Park beside the junction of the Great Northern main line and the branch to Highgate and Alexandra Palace in the late 1950s, a three-car Derby-built DMU heads for Kings Cross on the up local line on 14 October 1972. DMUs of this type had replaced some of the original Cravens units, as well as locomotive-hauled trains, on Great Northern suburban services in recent years.

Cravens diesel units were, however, still employed on such services until replaced by electric units in 1976/77. On 27 October 1972, a stopping train to Hertford North composed of these two-car units has just left Kings Cross suburban in the evening rush hour. On the left may be seen a typical array of main-line diesel locomotives in use on East Coast express services at this period.

This view taken from the window of one of the carriages of the down *Cambridge Buffet Express* on 10 December 1972 shows the demolition of the ramp to the former Highgate and Alexandra Palace branches, which took the down track, north of Finsbury Park station. The two tracks on the left are the down slow and down goods, which passed beneath the down Highgate track. Note also the semaphore signals still in use.

For several weeks in the spring of 1973, the Hertford Loop was closed to traffic while Ponsbourne Tunnel, north of Cuffley, was enlarged to accommodate overhead 25kV wiring for the forthcoming Great Northern suburban electrification scheme. London Country Bus Services Ltd provided a rail replacement service between Cuffley and Hertford North, using elderly ex-London Transport RT buses. Here on 11 March 1973, RT4550 awaits departure from Cuffley station for Hertford as an early Derby-built three-car DMU sets off for London. Note the early BR station sign on the left.

On the afternoon on Monday, 4 June 1973, Brush Type 2 (later Class 31) diesel, No 5592 hauls a rake of seven 1950s BR standard suburban carriages from Ferme Park sidings across the Great Northern main line just north of what was then called Harringay West station to take up service in the evening rush hour. The locomotive was one of those built in 1959/60 to replace N2 and L1 class tank engines on GN suburban duties; the carriages were of especially short length to negotiate the sharp Hotel Curve used by down suburban trains on the City widened lines from Moorgate to Kings Cross. Note also the large number of semaphore signals still in use.

On 28 July 1973, driving motor E51268 is at the trailing end of a formation of two Cravens two-car DMU units seen on an up local service at Welwyn Garden City. This particular car had been new to such services replacing steam in the late 1950s. Before too long, the footbridge here and at other stations along the line would be replaced as a result of overhead electrification. Welwyn Garden City would become the northern terminus for inner suburban GN electrics on the main line, as it still is today.

The previous photograph was taken from the window of one of the cars of this Cravens two-car unit, composed of driving trailer E56431 (leading) and driving motor E51301, heading for Baldock which was then usually the northern terminus for stopping services from Kings Cross. Again, both cars were new to these services, when for me, as a youngster of twelve or so, it was a great novelty to be able to sit behind the driver on journeys to and from Stevenage, where the train has just arrived here on 28 July 1973. The new Stevenage station, adjacent to the centre of the new town, has finally opened after many years of pressure from local residents. Note how it is still unfinished, with building materials on the platform – something that would never be tolerated by today's 'Health & Safety Gestapo'!

My train homewards that evening was the up *Cambridge Buffet Express*, hauled by Brush Type 2 diesel, No 5677. This was again a locomotive that had been new to these services. Note the planks of wood on the right – ideal 'ammunition' for vandals to place on the track and perhaps cause a derailment, although of course since the station was probably fully staffed at this period, the chances of that happening would have been remote.

On one of the platforms of Kings Cross suburban station, this Derby-built DMU formation is led by driving motor E50877. This was my mode of travel for another trip to Stevenage on 28 August 1973, and had been delivered in the mid-1950s for Western Region suburban services in the Birmingham area.

Seen from the same platform as the previous image, No 5614, a Brush Type 2 new to the GN suburban services, stands at the top of the platform which led up from Hotel Curve and the City Widened Lines. This platform had a pronounced slope, which once again would fall foul of Health & Safety regulations today.

At Stevenage station, Cravens driving motor E51267 is at the trailing end of a four-car formation terminating at Hitchin. The fact that it is on the down slow line suggests it has travelled via the Hertford Loop. Today, inner suburban electric trains on this route usually continue to Letchworth.

Seen from the bridge connecting the new town with Stevenage industrial area, Cravens driving motor E51294 leads a four-car formation on a stopping service on the up main line south of the station. The stretch of main line south of Langley Junction through Knebworth and Welwyn North has long been a bottleneck, still being only twin-track today.

On a wintry 12 January 1974, a two-car Cravens unit led by driving motor E51273 approaches Palmers Green station bound for Hertford North. Masts and overhead catenary have been erected ready for the inner suburban electrification. Note that tracks have been removed from the goods station on the right. The former goods yard on the left has already gone, and is apparently occupied by caravans just visible in the distance. Today a Morrison's supermarket occupies the site. When I took this photograph, I had no idea that I would move to Palmers Green in 1982, and still be living there in 2014!

The first day of service, 16 August 1976, for the Great Northern electrics which at first only ran in service between Drayton Park and Old Street. Here, new unit 313 017 crosses from the down (northbound) line to the up track to take up service for Old Street at Drayton Park. In November, full services began between Moorgate and Welwyn Garden City, and Hertford North or Letchworth. The southbound (up) ramp to the right had been built in 1939, to connect the Northern City Line to the main line at Finsbury Park, and then on via Crouch End to join London Transport's Northern Line at Highgate. But as we shall see later, it was not used for passenger services until November 1976! Most Class 313 units still operate the Great Northern suburban services today, but this one had been transferred to the North London Line and Euston – Watford services in the 1980s, and has ended up working along the south coast between Brighton and Portsmouth!

UNDERGROUND UNCOVERED

In many ways, London's underground railway has always been very different from the main-line railways even where trains run alongside or (as in the case of the Bakerloo and District Lines) share the tracks with former British Railways services. Passenger-carrying underground trains are interesting enough, but perhaps even more fascinating are the service locomotives which are used on engineers' trains, and often only used during the three or four hours when the system is closed in the early hours of the morning. Some are purpose-built others converted from redundant passenger-carrying rolling stock. In the period this book covers, some very old rolling stock still survived and remained in use.

The oldest electric rolling stock in use on the Underground at the time this book covers were electric sleet locomotives, used for de-icing conductor rails and tracks in cold weather. These were each converted from two Central London Railway electric locomotives dating from 1900. On 18 April 1970, loco ESL106 is one of two seen at Neasden depot.

Most engineers' trains on London's underground are hauled by battery-powered locomotives; their batteries being charged from the fourth rail when the current is switched on and then run on them when current is off. Here at Neasden depot on 5 August 1969 is a typical example, battery-powered locomotive L35, the first of the type, built in 1936 by the Gloucester Railway Carriage & Wagon Company with GEC electrical equipment. It is coupled to some flat wagons, used to transport replacement rails. The locomotive is on display at the London Transport Museum today.

At Neasden on the same day are two trailer cars of standard stock with a battery locomotive at each end of the formation. These were used to carry large numbers of 'gangers' to working sites when large-scale track or signalling equipment replacement was being carried out. The fact that they have doors at each end shows that these are later standard (pre-1938) stock, originally used when the Piccadilly Line was extended. They were in service for some thirty years use before being replaced by 1959 stock in the early 1960s.

Standard stock driving motor cars were also adapted for use as service locomotives, often as 'pilot motor cars' used for shunting in depots. An example of the type is seen outside Lillie Bridge depot on 23 August 1969. L69 is coupled to two flat wagons and a battery locomotive.

Battery locomotive L20 is one of a batch built by Metro-Cammell, also with GEC equipment, in 1964/65. The large building behind it is the Earls Court exhibition hall, used for many years for events such as the Motor Show. At the time of writing, it is due to be demolished to make way for a 'yuppie' housing development. The land that Lillie Bridge depot occupies is also threatened.

Battery locomotive L21, on 4 August 1970, hauls a four-car unit of 1960 stock through the disused Crouch End station. Thirty years earlier this should have become a Northern Line station on the extended Northern City service from Moorgate to Highgate, Alexandra Palace and East Finchley. Much work had been done to adapt this LNER branch for electric working, as we will see later, only for the scheme to be abandoned after the war. Passenger services ceased in 1954, with goods trains last running on the line until ten years later. After that, most ironically, this line between Finsbury Park and Highgate was used only to transfer tube stock to and from the isolated Northern City Line until late 1970.

Some of the Metropolitan Railway electric locomotives, which had hauled compartment stock trains from Liverpool Street and Baker Street to Rickmansworth before replacement by new 'A' stock units in 1961, were retained as shunting locomotives and to power engineers' trains on the District and Metropolitan Lines for a few years. Photographed at Ealing Common Depot in June 1972, locomotive No.5 retains its nameplate, *John Hampden*. This locomotive is now preserved as a static exhibit by the London Transport Museum.

WATERLOO SUNSET

As is well known, the former London & South Western main line from Waterloo to Southampton, Bournemouth and Weymouth was the last British main line passenger railway to retain steam haulage in the south of England. A combination of Southern Railway Bulleid Pacifics and BR Standard class locomotives, plus a handful of LMS Ivatt-designed 2-6-2Ts (albeit BR built), soldiered on until final replacement in July 1967, when the main line was fully electrified as far as Bournemouth. Since my office in County Hall was just across York Road from Waterloo Station, I spent many extended lunch hours photographing them in their final months, as well as travelling further down the line at weekends.

Typifying the final months of Southern steam, B.R. Standard 4-6-0 73085, originally named Melisande and one of those new to the South Western division only in 1957 to replace the original 'King Arthur' class, speeds south through Woking Station with a Bournemouth and Weymouth express on a very wet Whit Saturday, 27 May 1967.

On 15 January 1967, a gloomy Sunday, rebuilt West Country class No 34098 *Templecombe* awaits departure from Waterloo for Bournemouth. Its grimy condition typifies the way steam locomotives were being run down at this period, not just on the Southern Region, but also in the north on the London Midland and North Eastern regions. Many Bullied 'Pacifics' had been rebuilt in this form a few years previously, some only seeing three or four years' service before withdrawal. What a waste! I travelled behind *Templecombe* that day, in order to visit the engine shed and Bournemouth trolleybus depot.

RIGHT: Although less than 10 years old, BR Standard class 4MT 2-6-4T, No 80145 which had been built at Brighton Works in October 1956, is now one of several of this type used for shunting, empty stock and pick-up goods work in the London area of the former London & South Western Railway. Here, apart from the missing smokebox number plate, it still looks quite smart when leaving Waterloo on 16 February 1967 with a newspaper train taking copies of the *Evening News* and *Evening Standard* to stations down the line. However, four weeks before the end of steam, on 10 June 1967, a shortage of motive power saw No 80145 return to the sort of duty for which it had been designed. I travelled behind it on the 7.18am semi-fast to Salisbury, when it still managed to do about 60 mph, yet it would go for scrap a month later.

On 24 February 1967, two other BR Standard class 4MT 2-6-4Ts are both about to haul empty stock from arriving express trains out of Waterloo. The space to the left of the two engines would later be occupied by the additional platforms for *Eurostar* trains on Channel Tunnel services. How ridiculous that, at the time of writing, they have remained disused for nearly seven years following the transfer of these services to St. Pancras, whilst at the same time, Waterloo is crying out for additional capacity for domestic services!

A handful of L.M.R. class 2MT 2-6-2Ts also survived until the end of steam at Waterloo. Originally designed by Ivatt for the LMS, a number were built after nationalisation at Crewe Works. Photographed taking on water at Waterloo on 28 February 1967, No 41284 (built in November 1950) had gained fame by working the last steam-hauled Chesham branch shuttle for London Transport in 1961. That did not save it, as it was withdrawn at Nine Elms shed a few weeks before the end of steam. Others of the class, however, did survive to be preserved.

Caught from the window of a train on which I was travelling to Eastleigh on 12 March 1967, BR Standard class 4MT 2-6-0, No 76069 is shunting vans outside Woking station. As the number of serviceable steam locomotives declined, some of the class were used to haul boat trains to Southampton and Weymouth: but of course the 4MT was quite a powerful mixed-traffic locomotive, and in some cases only 9 or 10 years old.

A very strange spectacle at Waterloo on 23 March 1967 is that of No 80154, the last BR Standard class 4MT 2-6-4T of the 155 built, hauling a defective Bulleid 4-SUB EMU out of the terminus. The splendid Southern Railway signal box controlling the station and its environs forms a nice backdrop.

Entering the terminus with a string of vans on 27 March 1967, BR Standard class 3MT 2-6-2T, No 82029 at this time is one of just two survivors of the forty-five built. Although both remained in service until the end at Waterloo, both were scrapped and none have passed into preservation. The resemblance to the Ivatt-designed 2MT typifies how most BR Standard class locomotives were derived from LMS designs.

Similarly, the BR Standard class 5MT 4-6-0s had much in common with the LMS Stanier 5MT 'Black Five' 4-6-0s. Several of these survived on the main line to the southwest until the end, some having been specifically delivered to it in the late 1950s to replace elderly ex-LSW and SR King Arthur class 4-6-0 locomotives. They were often used on express services to Bournemouth and Weymouth in the final weeks, even on the *Bournemouth Belle*, when a Bulleid Pacific was not available. Photographed on 1 April 1967, outside the dilapidated Nine Elms shed, No 73022 undergoes attention to the smokebox.

A strange spectacle seen on 3 April 1967 as No 82019, the second survivor of the BR 3MT 2-6-2T class, approaching Vauxhall station from Waterloo hauling a string of seven vans and four Bulleid passenger express carriages! I presume it is not in passenger use, unlike the 'cattle trucks' (overcrowded commuter EMUs) to be seen there today! However, on the penultimate day of steam operation, one of these locomotives was pressed into passenger use!

On 5 April 1967, rebuilt Battle of Britain class No 34090, *Sir Eustace Missenden* departs from Waterloo in a cloud of steam when standing in for a Brush Type 4 diesel on the 12.30pm *Bournemouth Belle*. On the adjacent platform, Warship class D815 *Druid* is at the head of an Exeter train. Within five years, that too would be no more!

Ivatt 2MT 2-6-2T No 41319 hauling empties out of Waterloo on 5 April 1967. It had been to Eastleigh for maintenance in March before being transferred to Nine Elms shed, and was one of very few locomotives that had survived until the end of steam on the Southern to be preserved.

In the final weeks of steam, I often caught the Saturday 7.18am Waterloo to Salisbury to locations along the main line; for example the cutting at the junction with the Guildford line south of Woking. West Country class No 34023, *Blackmore Vale* drifts towards Woking on 20 May 1967, with an up semi-fast train of four carriages from Basingstoke. At this date, only three un-rebuilt Bulleid Pacifics remained in service. No 34023 has been preserved by the Bluebell Railway.

Another of these three survivors was No 34102 *Lapford*, which was kept in very smart condition at the small Basingstoke shed were it was based. Photographed on 22 May 1967 at Waterloo it is about depart with the 6.54pm semi-fast service to Basingstoke. Sadly, No 34102 went for scrap after the end of steam. Ironically, most of the others of this class which survive today had been withdrawn some two or three years earlier and were already in Woodham's scrapyard, Barry when this was taken!

BYGONE BAKERLOO

Today, the Bakerloo Line on London Underground is quite a simple affair, running from Elephant & Castle to Harrow & Wealdstone, with depots at London Road, Elephant, Queens Park and Stonebridge Park. However, until the spring of 1979, it was a much more complicated line, with trains continuing beyond Harrow & Wealdstone to Watford Junction, and also a separate branch from Baker Street to Stanmore, using tunnels built as part of the 1935-1940 New Works Programme, as far as Finchley Road: from there on taking over the former Metropolitan Line stopping service to Wembley Park and then on to the Stanmore branch. This latter section was taken over by the new Jubilee Line that opened in May 1979, while trains beyond Harrow were withdrawn in September 1982. Suggestions to reinstate the latter service have been made over recent years, perhaps it may yet happen.

Unique to the Bakerloo Line were the fifty-eight Standard Stock trailers adapted to run within 1938 tube stock units. They were known to staff as 'the 58 trailers'. One of these, No.70530, is seen in original condition at Queens Park station in May 1969.

When the Stanmore branch opened in 1939, the Bakerloo Line was provided with new 1938 tube stock. Unusually, however, many of the units were formed with one each of former Standard (pre-1938) stock trailers. A total of fifty-eight were built, leading to their nickname '58 trailers'. Two were rebuilt with end doors, and one of these, trailer 70518 is seen in Neasden sidings on 5 August 1969. This depot was shared with the Metropolitan Line, as it is today with the Jubilee Line which took over the Stanmore branch. As 1938 stock displaced from the Piccadilly and Northern Lines became available in the 1970s, these trailers were withdrawn but the main part of the Bakerloo Line retained 1938 stock units until November 1985.

Queensbury, one of two intermediate stations on the Stanmore branch, was upgraded with the new platform buildings ready for the takeover by the Bakerloo Line in 1939. The new branch quickly stimulated building development in the area, which in fact took its name from that given to the station, originally dreamed up as a partner to the existing nearby town of Kingsbury. Arriving at the station, on 9 May 1975, is 1938 stock driving motor car 11132 heading an Elephant-bound train.

LEFT: At Stanmore terminus on 4 April 1975, 1938 stock driving motor car 11076 heads a Bakerloo Line train bound for the Elephant& Castle. On the right, new sidings are being laid in preparation for the arrival of the Jubilee Line branch just over four years later. The station building, in the background, is built in typical Metropolitan Railway style of architecture. Ironically, the Metropolitan (and later London Transport) only operated this branch for seven years after it was opened in 1932. It was transferred to the Bakerloo Line in 1939 and thus has the distinction of having been served by three entirely different Underground lines! At the time when this image was taken, consideration was being given to extending this branch the short distance to Aldenham bus overhaul works; part of the facilities there would have been adapted for overhauling Underground rolling stock to replace the outdated Acton Works. This was indeed ironic, since Aldenham was originally to have been a depot and overhaul works for the Northern Line, as it would have been on its extension north of Edgware. Work on the extension was postponed as a result of the Second World War, and then abandoned after the conflict ended. However, the depot was built and adapted for the manufacture of Handley-Page Halifax aircraft, then converted for bus overhauling at the end of the war. Sadly in 1986, it was closed by the Thatcher regime and demolished a few years later.

In contrast, Kingsbury station had a more substantial building being built in typical Metropolitan Railway style. On the same day as the previous photograph, the next Bakerloo Line train to Elephant from Stanmore arrives with a 1938 stock driving motor car 11020 leading.

This '58 trailer', car 70518, is one of two that were modified with end doors. It is seen at the Bakelroo Line's Stanmore terminus, which had been taken over from the Metropolitan Line thirty years earlier, on the evening of 8 October 1969. Within ten years of this picture being taken, this terminus and its branch from Wembley Park along with the Bakerloo local service from there to Baker Street would be taken over by the new Jubilee Line.

WESTERN HYDRAULICS

Just as the Western Region's stud of GWR-designed steam locomotives were seen by their operators as a 'race apart' from those on the other regions of British Railways, so also were most of the first generation diesel locomotives built for the Western Region. Whereas all other BR regions had diesel electrics, the WR authorities at Swindon opted for diesel hydraulics. Following German practice, the first of these for express use were five Warship class built by North British in 1958, followed by thirty-three more built at Swindon between 1958 and 1961, another thirty-three of similar design from North British in 1960/61 and a then a final five from Swindon. These, particularly the first five, proved troublesome in service, but in late 1961, the more

successful Western class appeared from Swindon, totalling seventy-four locos in all. Production continued until 1964, the last forty-four being built at Crewe Works. Fifty-eight Type 2 diesels from North British, resembling the first five Warship class, were also built in 1959/60. Finally between 1961 and 1964, Beyer-Peacock delivered 101 Type 3 locomotives. Very similar to a batch of German diesels, these were usually referred to as 'Hymeks'. By the early 1970s, when spare diesel-electric locomotives had become available from other regions, the Western's diesel hydraulics were deemed to be non-standard, and despite Swindon's protestations, were rapidly withdrawn and all had gone by the end of the decade. Here we see some of them in their final years.

Some of the least successful and shortest-lived Western Region diesel hydraulic locomotives were the fifty-eight Class 2's built by North British in 1959. Here, at Paddington on 8 October 1967, D6328 still looks quite smart in B.R. rail blue livery when employed on empty stock working. These locos were already being withdrawn when this picture was taken.

On 30 December 1972, D1008 *Western Harrier* with the 2.30pm departure from Paddington gets up speed as it passes Royal Oak station.

Hymek 7001, the second of its class, brings a rake of empty carriages into Paddington for an evening rush hour departure on 17 April 1973. It is noteworthy that this class of diesel, along with the Western class, had raised metal numerals on the cab sides. Originally this would have included a 'D' prefix, but by 1973 this had been dropped by British Railways!

On the evening of 17 April 1973, D1030 *Western Musketeer* leaves Paddington with the 5.30pm departure. On the left is a Brush Type 4 (Class 47) diesel, the type that was used to replace the last main-line steam locos on the Western Region in 1964. The type also went on to replace many of the diesel hydraulics.

Hymek 7017, working empty stock that evening, awaiting the signal to leave Platform 1 at Paddington. This is one of four Hymeks that were preserved after the last of the type was withdrawn in 1975, and is in use on the West Somerset Railway today.

By now, the once mighty Western diesels were often demoted to menial duties. Here, approaching Southall station on the up slow line, D1027 *Western Lancer* is hauling what is probably a parcels train on 27 April 1973.

In contrast, D1067 *Western Druid* is still in express passenger use, heading towards Southall at the same location with a rake of BR Mk 2 carriages. To the left, a Hymek 7023 is on shunting duty in the goods yard.

Hymek diesel 7023 has moved out of the goods yard and is now slowly hauling a long string of trucks toward Southall station.

By 30 January 1976, only a few Western class diesel-hydraulic locomotives remained in use. Here, the second of the class built, D1001 *Western Pathfinder*, is well away from its old haunts heading west with a goods train as it crosses Edgware Road, Cricklewood, on the Dudden Hill loop. Today, seven Western class locomotives are preserved.

LITTLE AND LARGE!

Many people, even including railway enthusiasts unfamiliar with the London Underground system, do not realise that not all Underground trains are 'tube trains' and that many – those which worked the Circle, District, East London, Hammersmith & City and Metropolitan Lines in the years covered by this book – are built to virtually main-line loading gauge, and certainly could not fit in a tube tunnel! Similarly, people often do not realise that Underground trains share the same 4ft 8in tracks as main lines. The following photographs illustrate the point.

This view taken at Neasden depot on 6 June 1971 clearly shows the difference in size between Underground sub-surface stock and tube stock. Metropolitan Railway electric locomotive No.12 'Sarah Siddons', at the time used for brake block testing, contrasts with an electric sleet locomotive converted from Central London Railway cars. No.12 has since been preserved and is used to this day on enthusiasts' tours over the Underground's sub-surface lines.

In a view which clearly shows the difference in size between Underground tube and sub-surface stock, a train of silver tube stock speeds through Stamford Brook station on the Piccadilly Line non-stop fast tracks as another train of sub-surface District Line R stock waits. This is a very lucky shot for me, as the driving motor car at the trailing end of the eastbound Piccadilly Line train is car **1000**, indicating that this is the first 'silver' tube stock unit built for London Transport, and dated from 1956. This was the prototype for trains of 1959 and 1962 stock built for the Piccadilly and Central Lines, all finished in unpainted aluminium. Several of the R stock District Line cars, however, had originally been red, as will be explained later, and were painted silver to match newer unpainted aluminium-bodied cars.

RIGHT: At Whitechapel on 13 May 1973, a train of 1938 tube stock heads east on District Line tracks operating the 'Metro Tube Tour'. The difference in size between this and the train of C69 stock at the adjacent platform awaiting departure on the Hammersmith & City Line is obvious. The last C stock units have recently been withdrawn as this book is compiled.

Another view taken during the Metro Tube Tour on 13 May 1973 shows the train of 1938 tube stock, led by driving motor car 10093, heading south through Surrey Docks station on the East London Line, as a five-car train of sub-surface CO/CP stock calls there heading for Whitechapel. Once again, the difference in size is obvious.

Another image taken on 1 November 1975, which again emphasises the difference in size between London Underground surface and tube stock, shows a train of District Line CP stock headed by driving motor car 53226 departing from Barons Court station bound for Ealing Broadway, as 1959 stock driving motor car 1224 arrives on the adjacent platform bound for Rayners Lane on the Piccadilly Line. The District and Piccadilly Lines run alongside each other from this station to Acton Town.

SOUTHERN ELECTRIC

During the period covered by this book, several classes of pre-war Southern Railway electric-multiple units (EMU) were withdrawn and replaced by newer types. The replacement of some earlier post-war units also began. In this section are images of some of the older units that were so typical on the Southern Region in the 1960s and early 1970s.

Typifying pre-war Southern electric multiple units still in use in the late 1960's, 2BIL unit No.2135 is at the trailing end of an up semi-fast train on the Reading and Windsor lines passing through Richmond station on 9 May 1968. The B.R.C.W./Crompton type 2 Diesel on the left is an unusual visitor here, however.

Some of the oldest surviving Southern electric units still in use in the late 1960s were the 2BILs. Here at Woking station, on 6 May 1967, unit 2026 is at the trailing end of a six-car formation working an up semi-fast service to Waterloo. It was one of the second batch of these units built in 1936. The last 2BILs were withdrawn in 1971, but one unit has been preserved in working order. The designation '2BIL' denoted that there was a lavatory in each car. Car bodies were of composite construction, i.e. steel panelling on wooden frames mounted on steel underframes.

The 2HAL two-car unit was a development of the 2BIL, with a lavatory in only one car (HAL – Half Lavatory) and with all-steel bodies. They worked semi-fast as well as coastal services between, for example, Worthing, Brighton and Eastbourne. Here, unit 2665 arrives at Brighton station on 8 June 1968. The first of these units was delivered in 1939, and they remained in service until 1971.

Also at Brighton that day, 2BIL unit 2010 awaits departure. This was one of the first ten units of this type delivered in 1935. Note this unit, and the 2HAL on page 48, now has a yellow warning panel painted on the front. Some 2BIL and 2HAL units survived in service long enough to have an all-yellow cab front and to be painted in 'rail blue' livery.

For many years, the Bulleid-designed all-steel 4SUB class units worked the lion's share of suburban services on the Western Section, as well as on the Central and Eastern sections of the Southern Region. Units 4373 and 4620 are approaching Raynes Park, on 11 March 1973, with an up train for Waterloo. By now, the all-yellow cab front was an obligatory safety measure. Of the two units visible, 4373 was built by the Southern Railway; but 4620 was built after nationalisation. Apart from a prototype batch which was delivered during the war, all 4SUB units were built between 1946 and 1951.

Following on from the 4SUB units was the 4EPB, also designed by Bulleid, and designated EPB denoting electro-pneumatic braking. These operated suburban services mostly on the Eastern and Central sections of the Southern Region and were built by British Railways between 1951 and 1957. Later examples also classified as 4EPB units were built with standard BR Mk1 bodies until 1961. Unit 5247 is heading east out of Abbey Wood station on the North Kent Line on 28 March 1975. This level crossing was replaced by a bridge soon after this was taken, but EPB units remained in service for another twenty years. Unfortunately, although two units were restored in earlier liveries shortly before withdrawal, one has since been spilt with cars kept at two different preservation centres. The prototype unit 5001, which had been carefully painted in its original green livery, was scrapped in 2004 causing outrage among enthusiasts. In contrast, despite the last unit of the type having been withdrawn in 1983, a complete unit of the earlier 4SUB type is preserved in working order.

NORTH LONDON LINES

The North London Line of the London Midland Region of British Railways and the Northern City Line of the London Underground were the two railways most local to my original home in Canonbury Avenue: the two Highbury & Islington stations were just a short walk away.

This very wintry scene on 18 December 1971 shows a three-car unit of B.R. Eastleigh-built London Midland Region suburban stock (later termed Class 501) entering Gospel Oak station bound for Broad Street on the North London Line. The station has yet to have its platforms on this line shortened, whilst those on the former Tottenham & Hampstead Line are long disused. Note also the original signal box and the semaphore signals it controls. As this book is being completed, the two platforms seen here have been re-lenthened to take five-car London Overground trains, whilst one of the Tottenham & Hampstead ones was brought back into use in 1981 for trains to and from Barking via that line.

This view taken on 3 April 1968 shows the main entrance to Highbury & Islington Northern City Line station, situated on the north side of Holloway Road, opposite the LMR North London Line station. The latter was rebuilt to have a joint entrance with this station, which closed shortly after this was taken. Escalators, which replaced the original passenger lifts, and passages run beneath Holloway Road connecting the two buildings. The alterations were made as a result of the new Victoria Line serving the station. At the time this was taken, the exit and passageway from the rear of the lifts, to the right of the shop-front blind for 'Finlays', had become disused. The booking office was positioned to the left of the entrance. Recent years have seen plans to reopen this entrance, and the lifts for disabled access. However, the lift shafts only go down to an intermediate level. The frontage has recently been repainted and fitted with Underground display boards.

To facilitate interchange between the Piccadilly and Victoria Lines at Finsbury Park, the original Northern City Line Underground platforms were taken over for their southbound tracks, and the unfortunate Northern City, which had been intended to be extended from Finsbury Park to Highgate, Alexandra Palace, East Finchley and High Barnet, terminated at Drayton Park in October 1964. A replacement bus service from there to Finsbury Park was provided, but withdrawn when the first stage of the Victoria Line was opened on 1 September 1968. Here, a seven-car formation of 1938 Tube Stock awaits departure from Drayton Park for Moorgate on the evening of 5 August 1969. Not surprisingly, few if any passengers are to be seen.

LEFT: Taken the same day, this view shows the rear entrance to the station, with a splendid early London Transport sign still calling it 'Highbury' rather than 'Highbury & Islington'. Note also the sign above the entrance/exit saying 'Telephone'. There were telephone kiosks in the passage leading through to the lifts and booking office. Until 1969, we were not 'on the phone' at home, so if ever I was off sick from 'work', I had to be reported from them! Between them and the booking hall was an emergency staircase, the lower entrance to which, however, was cut off when the two new platforms were built to accommodate the northbound Northern City and Victoria Lines. Today, the staircase and lift shafts provide ventilation. To the right of the station, the building (then in use as a rather dubious 'night club' allegedly associated with the notorious Kray twins) was originally the Highbury Picture House, one of the first cinemas to open in Islington.

The junction at the northern end of Drayton Park station between the original Northern City Line southbound tunnel from Finsbury Park, and the new, ramped link to the surface at Finsbury Park built for the Northern City Line extension over the former LNER Northern Heights branches in 1939. As a result of the abandonment of the scheme in the early 1950s, the ramp was only ever used for transferring tube stock to and from the Northern City Line. It was finally brought into passenger use in 1976 when the British Railways Great Northern Electrics took over the line. As is evident here, the tunnel taking the ramp beneath the down BR track from the North London Line and Canonbury Tunnel to Finsbury Park was built only to tube-stock loading gauge, and had to be enlarged to accommodate full-size units. Note the wording at the side of the ramps describing the signalling still says 'Southbound from LNER'.

For more than thirty years, the exterior of Finsbury Park station was a rusting eyesore, giving the impression of a station that had been bombed during the war and never rebuilt! This was in fact the structural steelwork for an imposing façade, including a new booking office, and two additional platforms to accommodate the two tracks and an island platform for the Northern City Line's extension over the Northern Heights. Built to the east of the existing main line platforms, it also entailed demolishing buildings in Station Place. This view was taken on a dank 23 November 1969 and the structure was demolished a couple of years later. One of Finsbury Park's two bus stations occupies the site today.

Photographed on 23 March 1971, all that remains of the once grandiose Bow station on the North London Railway, (built near to the original headquarters of the railway) are seen partially demolished with what was the forecourt now on Bow Road. The station opened in 1850 but was rebuilt in this form in 1870, and even included a concert hall built in the upper storeys. Damage during the blitz caused passenger services to be withdrawn on this branch in May 1944, and a V-1 'doodlebug', that fell on the station a month later caused serious damage. However, it remained open as a parcels office until 1965, by which time the concert hall had been destroyed in a fire and demolished. The site was cleared in 1985, but in 1987, the path of the former North London Railway between here and Poplar came back to life in the form of the Docklands Light Railway, whose Bow Church station is on the opposite side of Bow Road to this original building.

A disused station in my local area which had actually seen use was Mildmay Park on the North London Line. It had been closed by the London, Midland and Scottish Railway in 1934. It was situated on the corner of Mildmay Park itself and Mildmay Grove, between Canonbury and Dalston Junction stations, and was built in the architectural style typical of the North London Railway. When this was taken on 8 January 1970, only a handful of such buildings still existed. Today, only Camden Road and Acton Central stations, along with the disused Hackney station which has recently been refurbished as a wine bar, survive. The building was demolished in the late 1970s when the adjacent bridge was rebuilt to accommodate overhead electrification. Just a few remnants of the station survive today at platform level.

A train of LMR North London Line Class 501 three-car electric stock loads up at Highbury & Islington bound for Richmond on 7 October 1972. Badly damaged during the Second World War, both during the 1940/41 blitz and then by a V-1 'doodlebug' flying bomb which fell on Highbury Corner on 27 June 1944, the platform buildings were rebuilt in 1957. A new booking hall was built ten years later, when it was linked to the adjacent Underground station. This latter work entailed the demolition of what remained of the original North London Railway frontage. During 2010/11, the platform buildings were completely rebuilt, other than the station house seen here on the extreme right and the 1950s canopy, to accommodate new London Overground services. The former 'steam' tracks, behind the fence on the left, are now used by trains on the North London Line proper (working today from Stratford to Willesden Junction and Richmond or Clapham Junction). At present, the two tracks seen here are used as the terminus for trains from London Overground's southern branches.

On 25 March 1972, a London Transport Routemaster bus squeezes gingerly beneath the railway bridge carrying the North London Line over Prince of Wales Road into Kentish Town West Station. At this period, the station seen under the arch on the left, most of whose structure was made of wood, had been burnt down by vandals, and was therefore closed. The bridge has claimed the 'lives' of many double-deck buses over the years, notably the prototype Class N1 trolleybus (No.1054) in 1960 and a Metroline 'Enviro 400' in more recent times. Route 46, which had only been introduced two months before this picture was taken, is worked by single-deckers today.

A L.M.R. Eastleigh-built three-car unit calls at what was then my local station, Highbury & Islington, on its way to Broad Street on 3 June 1972. Just visible are the new platform canopies provided when the station was partially rebuilt in the 1950's following wartime bomb damage.

A Class 501 unit at Bushey & Oxhey station on 13 May 1973 heading for Watford Junction. Note the pronounced curve to the platforms, something that would never do nowadays thanks to today's 'Health & Safety' nonsense; indeed reopening of the similarly-curved original Shoreditch Station on the resurrected North London Line south of Dalston was prevented for this reason! At the time this was taken, Class 501 units, which had replaced the original North London Oerlikon-built stock in 1957, were the mainstay of services from Broad Street to Richmond and Euston to Watford. Also there was still a service from Broad Street to Watford. All of these units, which were built at Eastleigh and similar to contemporary Southern Region EPB units, had been withdrawn by mid-1985.

FIRST-GENERATION DIESELS

The first main-line diesel locomotives were introduced by the London, Midland & Scottish Railway in late 1947, while each of the 'Big Four' main line railway companies had also purchased small 0-4-0 or 0-6-0 diesel shunters. British Railways continued with introducing the latter in its early years, and then in 1955 published a Modernisation Programme in which larger diesel locomotives were to replace steam on most main lines 'by about 1970', with diesel multiple units (DMU) working local suburban services and branch lines. Electrification was seen as the ultimate goal, and even now as this book is being compiled in the summer of 2014 has not yet reached the former Great Western main line west of London! Earlier BR diesel types are now referred to as 'first-generation diesels', and in the period this book covers were already beginning to be withdrawn and replaced either by newer types, or stock displaced by Beeching's savage cuts of the earlier 1960s, or by further electrification.

An early mid-1950's British Railways Derby-built diesel multiple unit loads up at the new Stevenage station with an all-stations 'stopper' to Kings Cross in the summer of 1973. DMU's similar in appearance to this were new to stopping services running from Marylebone, Paddington and St. Pancras during the period 1959-1962; those on the Great Northern suburban lines were originally Cravens two-car units, as seen elsewhere in this book.

These temporary awnings were erected after the sub-surface platforms of Moorgate station were burned out during the 'second Great Fire of London': the blitz of 29 December 1940. These two diesel locomotives typify those used for suburban services on the Great Northern and Midland main lines respectively, both of which traversed the Metropolitan Widened Lines from Kings Cross and St. Pancras to reach this city terminus. Earlier types had at first operated these services for a few months in 1958/59, but these are typical of those used throughout the 1960s and until electrification of these services in 1976/77 and 1983 respectively. Diesel multiple units also operated on both lines to Moorgate during those years. On the left is an Eastern Region Brush Type 2 new in 1960, and on the right we see a BR Derby-built Sulzer Type 2 new in 1962, during the evening rush hour on 3 April 1968. These later became British Rail Class 31 and 25 respectively, and although the latter had a short service life, a few type 31s are still running even today.

By following US-design practice, the two LMS prototype main-line diesels of 1947/48, and the 'Deltic' prototype which appeared in 1955, English Electric produced four types of main-line diesel locomotive for British Railways. The least successful of these were the Type 2 'Baby Deltics', of which ten were delivered in 1959 and used on Great Northern outer suburban services. By 1964, they had become so troublesome that they had to undergo major modification; but by 1969, most had been 'mothballed'. D5903 was one in a line of Baby Deltics photographed at Finsbury Park depot on 3 May 1969.

LEFT: During 1957/58, three classes of Type 1 diesel locomotives were introduced by British Railways for use on pick-up goods services, particularly on local branches. The first type was numbered from D8000 and built at Vulcan Foundry with English Electric-built engines. More than 200 of these were built over the ensuing ten years. This was followed by a batch of fifty British Thompson-Houston Type 1s, numbered from D8200 onwards, and final batch of ten built by North British, numbered from D8400. The latter two types were all allocated to the Eastern Region, mainly in the London area, but the NB-built examples were all withdrawn by the end of 1968, followed by those built by BTH. In the latter case, closure of branch lines and goods yards at local stations rendered the class redundant by 1971. On 3 May 1969, I photographed D8233, a surviving BTH type at Finsbury Park diesel depot. However, D8233 became static train electric-heating unit DB968000 after withdrawal, working for ten years or so in this capacity before being preserved. It is presently at the East Lancashire Railway. Meanwhile, the English Electric Type 1s, later known as the Class 20, became numerous throughout the London Midland, Eastern, North Eastern and Scottish Regions and some are still in use today.

The view looks north from the roof of the tower block at the North London Polytechnic. Two of the surviving BTH Type 1 diesels are crossing the bridge over Holloway Road on the Great Northern main line. In the foreground is what remains of the GNR Holloway Road station. This was closed in 1907 when what is now the Piccadilly Line station opened across the road, but the street-level booking office still exists. Today, only four tracks cross Holloway Road and two of the bridge spans have been removed. In the background, the high ground of Hampstead and Highgate is just visible.

Although main-line diesel locomotives were never used out of Marylebone (the former Great Central main line retained steam until closure in 1966 and used DMUs on its suburban services) they could be seen on goods or permanent way trains on that line. Photographed on 8 June 1969, D7587 a BR/Sulzer Type 2, one of the later examples of the class built in 1963, heads north from Harrow-On-The-Hill where the main-line tracks are electrified on the Underground's fourth-rail system.

The first production version of the English Electric main-line diesel to appear on British Railways in 1958 was the Type 4. A total of 200 were built, to run services on main lines out of Liverpool Street, Kings Cross and Euston. In the latter case they were a temporary measure until the electrification of the West Coast main line was completed in 1966. Here, 278 now finished in rail blue livery, calls at the old station at Stevenage on 12 October 1972, with the up Cambridge Buffet Express, which for some reason is running on the up slow line. The Type 4 later became the BR Class 40, and remained in service until 1985.

Best known of the English Electric main-line diesels was the Type 5 'Deltic'. Following the success of the prototype which appeared in 1955 then worked the West Coast and East Coast main lines on trials for the next four years, delivery of production examples began early in 1961. In effect, they replaced Gresley A4 Pacifics on top-link express work. Here 9003 *Meld* is between duties at Kings Cross on 27 October 1972. To the left, on the locomotive bank are a typical selection of early diesel types in use on East Coast main line at this period – a Brush Type 4, an English Electric Type 3, and a BR Peak Type 4. Deltics later became BR Class 55, and the last were withdrawn at the end of 1981. However, as well as the 1955 prototype, no fewer than six of the original twenty-two are preserved in working order.

As remarked earlier in this book, most of the Western Region's early diesels were different from those on other BR regions in being diesel hydraulics. Here on 30 December 1972, Hymek 7023 hauls the 3.00pm departure out of Paddington past Royal Oak station on London Transport's Hammersmith & City Line. By now, Brush Type 4 and English Electric Type 3 diesels, along with the later English Electric Type 4s in the D400 series (later known as Class 50) displaced by the northward electrification of the West Coast main line, were replacing all of these locomotives which were now regarded as non-standard by BR management.

LEFT: 6817 an English Electric Type 3 at Kings Cross on 27 October 1972. These first appeared working on the former Great Eastern main line at the same time as the first production Deltics early in 1961, and later became numerous on the Eastern, North Eastern and Western Regions. Several remain in use today. The design of the Type 3 contrasts sharply with that of the BR/Brush Type 4 (left), which first appeared in the autumn of 1962 and also still survives in main line use today.

In contrast to the Western Region's early diesel locomotives, the *Bristol Pullman* sets introduced in 1960 were diesel electrics, built by Metropolitan-Cammell and fitted with MAN engines. Driving motor car W60096 awaits departure from Platform 6 in the evening rush hour at Paddington on 17 April 1973.

In 1961, units which had originally been used to operate the *Midland Pullman* out of St. Pancras were transferred to the Western Region for the *South Wales Pullman* service. One of these, driving motor car W60092, leads the train through the complicated track work on the approaches to Paddington. The trains were withdrawn shortly after this photograph was taken, but the similarity between them and the new Inter-City 125 introduced a few years later is obvious. The 125s are still very much in express use today.

This unusual scene just west of Southall station on 27 April 1973 shows two early Western Region BR-built, BUT (Leyland)-engined DMU driving motor cars W50862 and W50915 in use as a parcels train and coupled to two general use vans. DMUs from the same batch were still in use on Great Northern suburban services in the London area at this period.

On the same day, Hymek 7023 shunts in the marshalling yard west of Southall station. Two BR/English Electric 0-6-0 diesel shunters are also in evidence. More than 1,000 of these were built between 1953 and 1963, with many remaining in use today.

The once 'mighty' Western class diesels were also being used to work goods traffic. Photographed on 27 April 1973, D1017 *Western Warrior* is approaching Southall on the up slow with what appears to be either a string of aggregate or coal wagons. By the end of the 1970s, all BR diesel hydraulics had been withdrawn.

Although usually associated with the Midland main line, BR Peak class 46 diesels also ran from Kings Cross on the East Coast main line to such places as Sheffield and Grimsby. Here 165, one of the later examples which later became BR Class 46, speeds north through the newly-opened Stevenage station on 28 July 1973.

The sidings at Poplar Dock on 4 October 1973: BR-built 0-4-0 Gardner-engined diesel shunter 2164 is one of a class of 200 introduced in 1957. By now, the docks were in terminal decline, rendering dock shunters like this redundant. Today, the Docklands Light Railway occupies much of the paths of the lines that once served the docks in this area.

On the same day, one of the larger and more numerous BR 0-6-0 shunters, 3309, hauls a string of coal trucks along the extensive sidings near Silvertown. The sidings fell into disuse a few years after this was taken; the Docklands Light Railway has taken over some of the earlier railway land in this area. The large building in the distance is the Tate & Lyle sugary refinery at Silvertown.

The Southern Region had the fewest first generation diesels, as of course much of its system was already electrified. However, the entire class of ninety-eight BRCW/Crompton Parkinson Type 3s delivered between 1960 and 1962 went to the Southern to replace an assortment of steam locomotives and were used on miscellaneous goods and, occasionally, passenger work. Here 6582 heads a permanent way train with a string of ballast wagons near Beckenham Hill station on 21 October 1973.

Brush Type 2 (Class 31) diesels were the backbone of Great Northern London suburban services for many years, until electrification in 1976/77. Here on 27 March 1975, 31226 heads a string of 1950s BR Mk1 short-wheelbase suburban carriages through Barbican station on a Widened Lines service into Moorgate.

Passing under a London Transport cable bridge, 31201 a Brush Type 2 enters Farringdon station bound for Moorgate, during the evening rush hour on 4 April 1975. Note the sign for National Car Parks Limited: this company used what was once the site of one of the goods yards. The tracks for the London Undergound's Circle/Hammersmith & City and Metropolitan Line are on the right.

A formation of three two-car Cravens DMUs, led by E56460 and E51295, depart from Farringdon for Welwyn Garden City on the same day. Once again, this type of DMU had replaced steam – in this case Gresley N2 tanks – on these services and they survived until the electrification of Great Northern inner suburban services in 1976. Note the war-damaged warehouses on the right. Offices occupy this site today, and Farringdon station has been enlarged to accommodate both the Thameslink services (which replaced the Midland suburban services in 1988) and Crossrail, which is due to open in 2018.

'Q' FOR QUAINT!

By the late 1960s, the oldest rolling stock in public service on the London Underground was the 'Q stock' running on the District and East London Lines. This terminology, in fact, related to a variety of types of rolling stock that had been inherited by London Transport from the District Railway, along with some that had been ordered by them but was delivered after the 1933 amalgamation of London's Underground railways. These were marshalled together in mixed formations, along with some cars of new Q38 stock delivered between 1938 and 1941. The oldest dated from 1923, yet these lasted as long as the newer cars. All were withdrawn from public service by early 1971.

During the period this book covers, most trains of Q Stock had at least one more modern, flared-sided Q38 stock car in their formations, but here at Putney Bridge station on 23 May 1970 this six-car District Line train that has terminated there is composed entirely of flat-sided, clerestory-roofed stock. By now, these units were being rapidly withdrawn from this line.

A former District Railway driving motor car of Q27 stock heads a mixed unit of Q stock bound for Dagenham East into Bromley-By-Bow station on 1 July 1969. Note, this car has flat sides and a clerestory roof, as on all earlier Q stock, but the next three cars behind it are Q38 Stock with flared sides which make them look much more modern. Cars of all types were indiscriminately mixed, and there were both driving motor cars and trailers of the Q38 type. Many of the latter had been originally designed with a view to converting them to driving motor cars. After the war many were converted to form the first of the R stock trains, also used on the District Line and reclassified R38, but many others remained as Q38s. It always struck me as odd that, when the older cars were time-expired, these newer Q38s were not formed into units of their own. Perhaps this was owing to an imbalance between the number of driving motor and trailer cars?

On the same day, Q23 stock driving motor car 4188 heads an Ealing Broadway-bound District Line train. These were the oldest cars of all still in service, dating from 1923 as implied by the classification. By now, all were marshalled at the western end of train formations which they gave a distinctly quaint and antique look.

At Whitechapel, the East London Line interchanges with, and runs beneath, the District and Hammersmith & City Lines. Here, also, two four-car formations of Q stock are seen working the East London Line on 1 July 1969. On the left, a Q27 driving motor car is at the trailing end of a train bound for either New Cross or New Cross Gate, while on the right an old Q23 driving motor car heads for Shoreditch. At this period, Shoreditch was served only during Monday to Friday rush hours (as here) and on Sunday mornings for nearby Club Row and the markets on Petticoat Lane. At other times, trains terminated at Whitechapel.

At Whitechapel the same evening, a driving motor car of Q27 stock is at the western (trailing) end of a District Line train bound for Upminster. Two other earlier cars are behind it, but then there is a Q38 car in the centre of the formation. Such mixing of types gave Q stock trains a distinctly odd appearance.

On the evening of 4 July 1969, a westbound District Line train approaches Hornchurch station. Headed by a Q38 driving motor car, the first three cars are Q38s, the next three are earlier clerestory-roofed Q stock, and the final two Q38s make up the eight-car formation. This typifies the use of odd stock.

The tour to celebrate the centenary of the District Railway/District Line took place on 24 August 1969. Here, with a Q23 driving motor car leading the formation, it passes through the former District Railway Boston Manor station bound for Hounslow West. District Line trains ceased serving this section in the autumn of 1963, leaving it solely to the Piccadilly Line which had been extended over it some thirty years earlier. In this view, the original District Railway platform buildings, and the new Chas. Holden-designed booking hall built for the Piccadilly Line extension, may be seen.

Although East London Line Q stock trains were only four-car units, these also used mixed formations. A Q38 driving motor car, at New Cross Gate on 6 September 1969, is attached to three earlier cars.

An elderly Q23 stock driving motor car heads a four-car formation of East London Line Q stock at its other southern terminus, New Cross on 6 September 1969. It is not really bound for Olympia, but only going to Whitechapel – the driver, Richard Evans, has put that destination plate up for a joke! It is worth noting that these cars had the metal destination plates mounted on external brackets, whereas those on Q27 and Q38 cars were mounted internally behind a glass screen.

This interior view of the same Q23 car (4204) shows the comfortable, deep-cushioned seating, arranged as a mixture of peripheral and transverse seats which was normal practice on the Underground. A far cry from the dreadfully hard, peripheral-only seating on today's Class 378 units of London Overground on the East London Line, and also the new S stock trains on the Circle, District and Hammersmith & City Lines.

THE
ODD SPOT

Something that has always made railway photography even more interesting is the existence, or appearance, of unusual rolling stock, or unusual workings.

An oddity to be seen on the main line between Victoria and Brighton on 8 June 1968 is No.20001, one of the two Bulleid-designed Co-Co electric locomotives built in 1941 for the Southern Railway. Here it has arrived at Brighton and is 'changing ends' when propelling the Bulleid Commemorative Railtour that day.

The section of District Line between Wimbledon and East Putney is often used by main-line rolling stock running from the former Southern Region's Durnsford Road depot, Wimbledon and the Windsor and Reading lines with which there is a link at East Putney. Here on 4 August 1969, an elderly ex-Southern Railway 2BIL unit (2082) passes through East Putney's two disused platforms on the link. Note also the BR Southern Region totem sign on the right – this region still managed the line from here to Wimbledon at the time.

Photographed on 7 August 1969, this train formed of London Transport 1938 tube stock looks as if it is in normal service. However, it is not. The three-car unit is being towed by a battery locomotive, which is just visible at the far end, and is crossing the Great Northern main line at Finsbury Park on the way to Highgate. This is one of the weekly stock transfers between the Northern Line's Highgate depot and the isolated Northern City Line at Drayton Park. To do this, trains traversed the Highgate to Finsbury Park branch which should have become part of the Northern Line in 1940. On the right is the original footbridge crossing over the main line.

A former Central Line train formed of 1960 tube stock has recently been adapted as a track testing unit and is passing through Acton Town station on 7 August 1969. Originally it retained its two pre-1938 (Standard) stock trailers, but in the 1980s a 1973 stock car was acquired to replace them. The train is still in use at the time this book was being compiled.

A chance sighting on 7 August 1970 at Finsbury Park when I was waiting for the Highgate to Drayton Park tube stock transfer to appear was 'Baby Deltic' D5908 heading north on the down fast line with a goods train. By now this was the only survivor of the ten built, and it was also the only one to be finished in British Rail 'rail blue' livery. It was withdrawn in 1971.

A real oddity seen in October 1970 at the Ealing Common depot of the District Line is this tube stock driving motor car. Although it looks like a 1938 stock car, it is in fact one of the 1935 experimental streamlined cars that had been modified to run with 1938 stock. After being used for a few years on the Epping to Ongar shuttle service on the Central Line, two cars, including this one, were used in experiments to see whether it was feasible to operate articulated units on the Underground. However, nothing came of this and they were later scrapped.

A train of District Line CP stock heads eastbound into Farringdon station during September 1972. At this time, some District Line trains ran around the north side of the Circle Line through here on Saturdays, rather than around its southern section via Victoria. By now, trains of this type had been replaced on the Circle and Hammersmith & City Lines by new C stock, so were not usually seen in service at Farringdon at this time.

A very late pre-nationalisation survivor was ex-LNER Gresley buffet car E9122E. Finished in current BR express blue and grey livery it, along with another elderly Thompson buffet car, was retained for use on the *Cambridge Buffet Express*. On 9 September 1973, the coach was in Bounds Green carriage sidings, to the east of where the Hertford Loop leaves the Great Northern main line. Today, this is the location of the depot for HSTs used on the main line.

Oddities on the Central Line of London's Underground were the units of 1960 tube stock, at this period confined to the Hainualt to Woodford shuttle service and equipped for automatic train operation. Here on 2 July 1971, one of them is seen leaving Chigwell Station for Hainault. The unit's two trailers are modified standard stock cars.

During 1974/75, the East London Line was worked by 1938 tube stock cars. They were maintained at Neasden depot (which had them for the Bakerloo Line), and stock transfers took place between the East London's New Cross depot and Neasden, by way of St. Mary's Curve and the Hammersmith & City Line to Baker Street, and then the Metropolitan main line. 1938 Stock driving motor car 10098 is at the trailing end of one of these units about to enter the tunnel north of Baker Street station on 9 March 1975. Subsequently, A Stock units from the Metropolitan Line were used on the East London Line and, with the exception of a period in the early 1980s when new District Line D stock was used, were transferred using this route until the line closed for alteration to become part of the London Overground network at the end of 2007.

RIGHT: An early Brush Type 2 diesel 5507 running with an engineers' train, (involved in the replacement of the railway bridge over Mare Street), just east of the then-closed Hackney station on the North London Line on 15 September 1973. Passenger services on this line east of Dalston were withdrawn as a result of wartime bombing, but were restored in May 1979, initially without intermediate stations between Canonbury and Stratford. Stations at Dalston Kingsland, Hackney Central, Homerton and Hackney Wick were reinstated between 1980 and 1985. The line now forms part of the busy London Overground network on the North London Line between Stratford, Willesden Junction, Richmond and Clapham Junction. In the foreground are prefabricated (prefabs) housing built to replace the many houses in the area destroyed by wartime bombing.

Southern Region electro-diesel E6003 is about to pass over the level crossing with an engineers' train at Merton Park station on 2 October 1973. Instead of heading along the Southern branch from Wimbledon to West Croydon, however, it is for some reason about to go on Merton Abbey branch. This branch was closed to passenger services in 1929, but goods services continued along part of it until 1975. Ironically, they served the Triang toy factory which made model railways! Meanwhile, the line to West Croydon has since become part of the Croydon Tramlink system which opened in 2000.

An oddity to be seen for many years on the Northern Line was 1938 stock driving motor car 10306. It was rebuilt after wartime bomb damage with most of its windows extending into the roof in an effort to improve passenger visibility. This idea proved a success and was adapted for the new 1967 stock tube trains built for the Victoria Line, and the subsequent 1972 and 1973 stock trains. Here we see it in the middle of a 1938 stock train at Brent on 31 March 1975. This station was renamed Brent Cross following the opening of the shopping centre in 1976.

New units of Victoria Line 1967 tube stock, also A.T.O. fitted, were run in on the Hainault to Woodford shuttle at this period. One of these is seen in Chigwell station, which is still in original Great Eastern Railway condition, on 2 July 1971. Use of these units ceased on this line three weeks later, when all available units of this type were needed for the Victoria Line's newly-opened extension to Brixton.

SILVER SERVICE

Silver or to be more correct, unpainted aluminium, trains were first introduced on to the London Underground in the 1950s, in the form of the prototype 1956 stock tube cars on the Piccadilly Line and of some of the newer R stock sub-surface cars on the District Line. Judged to be a success, new unpainted cars were then specified for the 1959, 1960 and 1962 tube stocks for the Piccadilly and Central Lines, the A Stock for the Metropolitan Line, 1967 tube stock on the Victoria Line, C Stock for the Circle and Hammersmith & City Lines, 1972 tube stock for the Northern Line, 1973 tube stock for the Piccadilly, D Stock for the District Line and finally the short-lived 1983 tube stock on the Jubilee Line. Additionally, all R stock cars which had originally been red were painted in a silver/white livery to match their newer unpainted cars on the District Line. However, by the mid-1980s, a combination of wear and tear, the scourge of graffiti, and laxer maintenance under Thatcher's London Regional Transport regime meant most cars had become a dirty grey, rather than 'silver'. Thus subsequent deliveries were painted in a new livery of red, white and blue and earlier trains of A, C, D, 1967, 1972 (Mk II) and 1973 stock painted the same.

Seen from the road bridge to the north of Oakwood Station on 26 March 1970, a train of 1959 tube stock goes through the car wash at the southern end of the Piccadilly Line's Cockfosters depot. This unit typifies 'silver' tube stock units which comprised most of the Central and Piccadilly Line's trains during this period.

The first 'silver' sub-surface
stock Underground trains
were the District Line R stock,
a train of which is working
westbound at Barking on 4
July 1969. Many of these cars
were Q stock trailers built in
1938-1941 and converted to
driving motors after the war.
Others were newly built to the
same general (1938) design
after the war in 1947 and
1949, and one small batch
was built as late as 1959.
The last R Stock trains were
withdrawn in the spring of
1983.

The smallest class of 'silver' cars operated on the London Underground was the 1960 tube stock, of which new unpainted aluminium driving motor cars were supplied by Cravens to run with reconditioned pre-1938 Standard stock trailers (painted silver) on the Central Line. Owing to the pressing need to replace the line's ailing fleet of Standard stock cars more quickly, once new electric trains had replaced steam on suburban services out of Liverpool Street in November 1960, and also because the reconditioning of the old trailers was proving more difficult than anticipated, only five, four car-units of 1960 stock were delivered. Instead, a repeat order for 1959 tube stock cars (deemed to be 1962 stock eventually) for the Central Line, which in the meantime had those intended for the Piccadilly Line at first, was made. The 1960 units were then used for automatic train operation trials, in anticipation of this being used on the Victoria Line, on the Woodford to Hainault shuttle service of the Central Line. Here, 1960 driving motor car 3904 arrives at Hainault on 7 August 1969. Note the new buildings provided at the time the Central Line replaced the former LNER steam services on this line, whereas the platform on the right still has the original Great Eastern buildings.

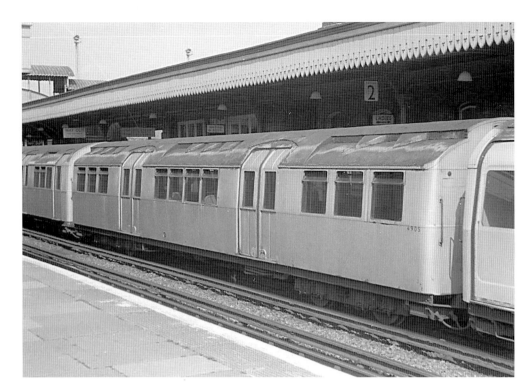

The same train at Woodford, and we see the two Standard Stock trailers it contains. Car 4905 is an earlier example, without end doors, whereas 4904 is a later type, which does have end doors. Later in their lives, the 1960 stock units had these elderly trailers replaced by 1938 stock trailers and, ironically, for their last few years when working both the Woodford to Hainault and Epping to Ongar shuttles, the trains were painted red.

As mentioned above, most of the Central Line's new trains were of 1962 stock, which was virtually identical to the unpainted 1959 stock on the Piccadilly Line, built by Metro-Cammell. Here on 29 August 1973, driving motor car 1641 is at the trailing end of a formation of two four-car 1962 stock units leaving Debden for Epping. Ironically, these newer units were all withdrawn from the Central Line by mid-1995 and only a handful of survivors had been transferred to the Northern Line which by then had most of the 1959 Stock. The last units of this type were withdrawn in January 2000. This view shows the original Great Eastern platform buildings on Debden's down (eastbound) platform. Those on the up (westbound) platform were rebuilt upon the Central Line's takeover of the Epping and Hainault branches, which had been delayed due to the war but were electrified in the late 1940s. This station was originally named Chigwell Lane.

Problems with ailing 1938 tube stock on the Northern Line in the early 1970s led to its being dubbed 'The Misery Line'. In an attempt to remedy the situation, two batches of new tube cars were ordered from Metro-Cammell to augment services. Built to the same general design as the 1967 tube stock on the Victoria Line, but adapted for crew operation, these became known as 1972 Mk 1 and Mk 2 tube stock. Here on 4 January 1975, 1972 Mk 2 driving motor car 3561 heads a train that has just turned short at East Finchley station, on one of the centre platforms that should have accommodated trains from Moorgate and the Northern City Line via Finsbury Park and Highgate. This station was completely rebuilt in 1939/40 as part of the 1935-1940 New Works Programme and should have afforded interchange between this line and 'main' Northern Line.

Following on from the 1972 tube stock cars, the 1973 stock fleet was delivered to replace 1959 stock on the Piccadilly Line, which moved to both the Northern and Bakerloo Lines, eventually ending up on the Northern. Here on 19 February 1975, the first complete train of this type, headed by driving motor car 100, heads out of Acton Works past Acton Town station for a test run. In common with the 1972 Mk 2 units, these cars were refurbished in the 1990s. They comprise the entire rolling stock of the Piccadilly Line today, and will see service well into the 2020s.

On 4 April 1975, a train of 1972 Mk1 tube stock leaves Woodside Park station on the Northern Line's High Barnet branch for the south. Most trains of this type remained on the Northern Line until their final withdrawal in January 2000. Woodside Park is another former Great Northern Railway station that is still in virtually original condition. Fortunately, electrification of this branch was well enough advanced to open in April 1940 before work on other parts of the Northern Line's extension over former GNR/LNER branches in North London stopped.

At the Piccadilly Line's northernmost terminus, Cockfosters, driving motor car 1308 heads a train of 1959 tube stock bound for Rayners Lane on 8 May 1975. By now, as may be seen on its cab front, these trains were becoming more 'dirty grey' than 'silver', but they soldiered on for almost twenty-five years longer. As is obvious, their design was derived from that of the 1938 stock, and apart from being 'silver' rather than red, and having slightly different cab fronts and interior layouts for their transverse seats, were indeed almost identical.

Still looking quite smart, R38 driving motor car 21125 is at the trailing end of a formation of District Line 'silver' R stock heading for Barking when seen at Earls Court on 1 November 1975. In common with many of its type, this had originally been a Q38 trailer and was rebuilt as a driving motor car after the war. Such cars could be distinguished from those built new as R stock by having four windows between their double doors, whereas the newer cars had two larger windows instead.

On the same day as the previous photograph, driving motor car 1224 heads a train of Piccadilly Line 1959 tube stock which has just terminated at Rayners Lane, then the usual off-peak terminus for trains on this line on the Uxbridge branch. As may be seen by the typical Chas. Holden buildings in the background, this station which is at the junction of the Metropolitan Line Uxbridge branch (from Harrow) and the former District Railway branch from Acton Town, was completely rebuilt when the Piccadilly Line took over the latter in 1932. Forty-five years later, new units of 1973 tube stock replaced 1959 stock.

STATIONS ACROSS LONDON

As will be obvious, the hundreds of railway stations throughout the London area have vastly varied histories, ranging from the major main-line termini to small, country stations which are little more than halts. Their origins and architecture are just as fascinating as the rolling stock that serves them, and in this section we take a look at some of them, both closed and still in use, as they were in the period covered by this book.

This view taken on 20 June 1970 shows the former Metropolitan Railway Marlborough Road station on Finchley Road. It was closed in 1939 upon opening of the new Bakerloo Line stations at Swiss Cottage and St. John's Wood a short distance away. When this picture was taken, the building was up for lease. Its booking office became a Chinese restaurant, which it still is today. However it still has emergency access to and from platform level.

Taken at Waterloo in April 1967 looking beyond Platform 21, to the sidings that were situated between it and York Road. A notable feature here was a hoist for bringing cars from the Waterloo & City Line to the surface. In this view, a Bulleid-designed 4EPB unit awaits departure for Windsor Riverside; one of the many BR Standard class 4-6-0s used on the South Western lines of the Southern Region simmers away shunting goods wagons. In the background are the ugly 1950s office blocks which replaced blitz-damaged buildings along York Road. All of these sidings were swept away when the terminus for the Channel Tunnel Eurostar services was built in the early 1990s.

Without doubt the most outrageous disused surface station in the whole of Greater London is Highgate (High Level). This was completely rebuilt in 1940 as a modern, London Transport surface station to serve Underground trains on the Northern City Line's extension from Finsbury Park to Highgate, Alexandra Palace, East Finchley and High Barnet. Sadly, as related elsewhere in this book, this extension was never completed but it was used by BR local trains until 1954. Here on 15 June 1969, I inspect what is left of some BR posters.

The next station southwards on the branch was Crouch End, whose boarded- and bricked-up booking office stood on the bridge over the line at the top of Crouch End Hill. Similar to those on other Great Northern branches in the North London area, it was demolished in 1978 to obviate a weight restriction on the bridge. However, the platforms here remain. This view was taken on 5 August 1969.

A smartened-up Q23 stock driving motor car leads the District Line's *Centenarian* tour through Rickmansworth station, on 24 August 1969. This station, built originally by the Metropolitan Railway and served later by the Great Central Railway and its successors' expresses, should have been rebuilt and the line four-tracked under London Transport's 1935-1940 New Works Programme, but like the uncompleted Northern Line extensions seen above, work was placed in abeyance during the war. When it was resumed in the late 1950s, its scope was scaled down and the station remained in largely original condition, as it is today. The ornate ironwork on the platform buildings is of particular note.

Moorgate station was very badly damaged during the blitz of 29 December 1940. During that raid, a train of O/P stock was completely burnt out, with its aluminium and steel body shells completely distorted. Here, in September 1969, the 'temporary' platform buildings erected afterwards for the through sub-surface Circle and Metropolitan Line tracks are still in use, while new offices rise above the station on the left. Today, it is completely built over by office development. Here, two CO/CP units are seen in the station. Nearest the camera is one of the District Line Saturday trains that ran to Wimbledon via the northern side of the Circle Line (i.e. via Kings Cross) at this period.

A long-closed station whose booking office still survived when seen on 8 November 1969 was the former GWR Uxbridge High Street station. This was the terminus of a branch from Denham, on the Great Central & Great Western joint line, with which it had a triangular junction. It had originally been intended to continue the line beyond here to link with the GWR's other branch in Uxbridge, at Vine Street, thus forming a loop back to the main line at West Drayton, much in the way the Greenford Loop links the two former Great Western main lines. This explains why the line terminated on a viaduct, since to form the loop, it would have had to cross the High Street and in fact a bridge was built across this thoroughfare, now known as the Oxford Road. However, this was not to be, perhaps owing to competition from the Metropolitan Railway. The branch had opened in 1907 and lost its passenger service shortly after the outbreak of the Second World War. Goods services continued until July 1964. At the time this was taken the coal merchant's office was still in use. The buildings were demolished in the early 1970s.

Another long-closed London station still extant at this time was City Road, between Angel and Old Street on the City & South London Railway. This was closed in 1922 when the line was modified to take normal tube stock trains and linked with the Edgware, Highgate & Morden Line (later the Northern Line). The building is on the corner of City Road and Central Street, and part of it survives today as a ventilation and emergency access shaft. Its platform spaces are used for storage.

This Christmas card-like scene was in fact taken on 26 December 1970, from the footbridge at the London end of Crouch End station, which had been closed in 1954 after plans to extend the Northern City Line through it from Finsbury Park to Highgate and Alexandra Palace had been abandoned. Tube stock transfers through it, on the up line only, had ceased some two months before, and tracks were finally lifted a few months later. As may be seen on the down track, on the left, this was fouled by a support for the weak bridge beneath the former booking office. That was demolished in 1978, and the platform buildings, which extended most of the length on both sides, had already gone in 1967. Only the track bed and platforms survive today.

Also on the Northern Line, this view of the street-level entrance to Strand station on the Charing Cross branch was taken on 15 April 1973. Originally on the Hampstead tube, the station was enlarged and combined with the adjacent Bakerloo Line Trafalgar Square station when the new Jubilee Line opened with its terminus there in May 1979, and renamed Charing Cross. This entrance was closed shortly after this was taken, with new accesses to it via a sub-surface booking hall direct from Charing Cross main line station (seen behind the Strand entrance on the left) and an entrance on the north side of the Strand. To confuse matters, both the Bakerloo and Northern Lines already had stations called 'Charing Cross' with interchange to the Circle and District Lines a short distance away.

This view at Farringdon station taken on 13 May 1973 shows the ornate glass roof which was damaged during the war and never properly reinstated. A train of 1938 tube stock, headed by driving motor car 10093, heads west on the 'Metro Tube Tour' along the Circle and Metropolitan Lines. The City Widened Lines, served at the time by diesel trains from the Midland and Great Northern suburban lines, are on the right. In recent years, as mentioned earlier, Farringdon station has been given a splendid new roof and enlarged.

All of the stations on the High Barnet branch of the Northern Line, except for East Finchley, retain their original Great Northern Railway buildings. A splendid example is the station house at Woodside Park, photographed on 4 April 1975. The structure to the right is a footbridge crossing the track which is at street level at this point. Most of the stations on the former Great Eastern and Great Northern branches taken over by the London Underground from the London & North Eastern Railway as a result of the 1935-1940 New Works Programme, on the Central and Northern Line, retain their original buildings. More's the pity that not all those on the Northern opened as Underground stations.

The only surface station on the Great Northern & City Railway (later the Northern City Line) was Drayton Park, although its platforms are still in a deep cutting. This view taken on 20 April 1975 shows the booking office a few months before the line was given over by London Transport for conversion to accommodate the Great Northern electrics, where their line comes to the surface. Note the LT 'bullseye' sign to the right.

In contrast to the former Great Northern suburban stations taken over by the Northern Line in 1940/41, many of those on the Great Northern main line were drastically rebuilt when the inner suburban services were electrified in 1976/77. One of these was then called Wood Green (for Alexandra Park), the junction of the main line and the southern end of the Hertford Loop. This view looking north, taken on 2 September 1976, shows a Cravens two-car DMU departing for Hertford North, as the brand new EMU 313019 heads south on the up slow line. The latter units took over inner suburban services two months later, and still operate these today. All the platform buildings at this station were demolished in preparation for the electrification. The bridge carrying Bridge Road over the railway and the station footbridge had to also be rebuilt. However, the original booking office on the up side in Station Road was retained. The station was renamed 'Alexandra Palace', by the then famous actress Diana Dors in 1982. More recently, an extra platform has been reinstated on the up side for the long-delayed 'Thameslink 2000' programme which will finally see the former Great Northern suburban services linked with the Thameslink network in 2018.

DISTRICT DIVERSITY

The District Line of the London Underground had the greatest diversity of rolling stock during the period this book covers. It had, and still has, one of the most complicated service patterns on the system, with the eastern section reaching distant Upminster, and its western branches terminating at Ealing Broadway, Richmond and Wimbledon, as well as a service from the latter to Edgware Road and the shuttle service to Olympia.

This view taken at Barking sidings on 4 July 1969 illustrates some the different types of unit in use on the District Line at the time. Four cars of District Railway Q stock are in the foreground, with a train of more recent CO/CP stock behind them.

As we saw previously, the District Line operated trains of mixed Q stock at this period. Here at Bromley-By-Bow on 4 July 1969, a modern Q38 stock driving motor car is at the trailing (western) end of a formation of these cars bound for Upminster. The remainder of the cars in the train are older, flat-sided clerestory-roofed cars. Despite being newer, the Q38 stock cars were withdrawn at the same time as the older ones, and all had gone by the spring of 1971. Meanwhile, the booking office of this station was replaced early in 1970 in conjunction with GLC road improvements connected with the northern approach to the Blackwall Tunnel and Bow Bridge flyover.

It had been intended to marshal all Q38 stock cars into trains of new R stock, but in the event it was not always done which explains why many survived in mixed formations (above) for so long. Those that were done comprised many trailer cars which were converted to driving motor cars and formed into trains of R Stock with new cars after the war. These were the first 'silver' trains on the Underground, though most were painted rather than being delivered in unpainted condition. An example of such a train is seen heading east of Barking for Dagenham East on 4 July 1969. Barking sidings are just visible in the distance.

An elderly Q23 car heads a mixed formation of Q stock bound for Wimbledon as it approaches Hornchurch station on 4 July 1969. A Q38 stock driving motor car is just visible at the rear.

Bound for Wimbledon, a train of Q stock headed by a Q27 driving motor car arrives at Gloucester Road station on 18 July 1969. Shared with the Circle Line, these sub-surface platforms at this station have since been roofed over by office development. At this time, the tracks here had an unusual arrangement, in that the left-hand track was for 'outer rail' (clockwise) Circle Line trains, with eastbound District Line trains and those on the Circle 'inner rail' (anti-clockwise) service using a third platform (out of the picture) on the left. Subsequently, the centre island platform was widened and the eastbound track taken out of use, and replaced by what had been the westbound Circle Line platform, i.e. that on the left. A shopping mall and flats were also built above these platforms in the 1990s.

A third type of unit, albeit featuring the same flared-sided body style as the Q38 and R stock, working District Line services in 1969 was the CP stock. A seven-car formation of this arrives at East Putney on the Wimbledon branch on 4 August 1969. These units had previously operated Metropolitan Line services to Uxbridge and were replaced by new A stock in 1962/63. Further trains of this type (and the similarly-bodied CO stock) replaced by new C stock on the Circle and Hammersmith & City Lines would replace the last Q stock on the District and East London Lines in 1970/71.

A Q27 car at the trailing end of an Upminster-bound train at West Brompton station on 4 August 1969. At the time, only District Line services between Wimbledon and Edgware Road or Upminster served this station, but in June 1999 the adjacent platforms on the West London Line were reopened, to provide interchange with Southern trains running from Milton Keynes and Watford to stations on the Brighton main line, and also the 'Silverlink' Willesden Junction to Clapham Junction service. This latter has now become part of the London Overground network, its trains providing an alternative service to East London by running to Stratford.

When the Piccadilly Line was extended west of Hammersmith in 1932, the District Railway was four-tracked as far as Acton Town, and their trains worked the outer two tracks and stopped at intermediate stations: the Piccadilly service usually ran non-stop between Hammersmith and Acton Town using the inner two tracks. This meant that new eastbound platforms for the District trains had to be built on the north side of the tracks. An Upminster-bound train headed by a Q27 driving motor arrives on one of these platforms at Stamford Brook on 4 August 1969.

This view on the northbound platform of East Putney station, taken on 4 August 1969, shows that semaphore signalling was still in use on the Wimbledon branch of the District Line which was still managed by the Southern Region. Note the passenger-controlled door-operating buttons, deactivated some years earlier, on this train of Q stock.

This Upminster-bound District Line train at East Putney, on 4 August 1969, is unusual for the time in having all eight cars marshalled with flat-sided, clerestory-roofed Q stock cars. Note the SR-style six or eight car stop sign on the left, and the ex-LSWR signal cabin on the right.

The eastern section of the District Line, between Bromley-By-Bow and Upminster, was also managed by BR Eastern Region at this time. Here, an elderly Q23 driving motor car is at the trailing end of an Upminster-bound District Line train departing from Plaistow, as a BR electric unit speeds by on the London, Tilbury & Southend main line to Fenchurch Street. Such trains had long ceased to call at such intermediate stations, although they have stopped at West Ham since May 1999 when a platform was reinstated there to allow interchange with the Jubilee and North London Lines.

Specially cleaned to work the *Centenarian* tour, a Q27 driving motor car leads the train through Park Royal station on its way from Uxbridge to Acton Town on 24 August 1969. This branch of the District Line had been taken over by the Piccadilly Line in 1932, and most of the stations were substantially rebuilt.

At this period, some District Line trains terminated from the north at Putney Bridge station. Here a six-car train composed entirely of clerestory-roofed, flat-sided Q stock cars stands in one of the terminal platforms on 29 September 1969. A gantry of semaphore signals is just visible in the background

A train of CO stock heads west, under a cable bridge, out of Farringdon in September 1972. The destination 'Circle Line, District' is somewhat confusing – the train is in fact a District Line service running from Upminster to Wimbledon via Kings Cross and the north side of the Circle Line. As mentioned earlier, during this period some District Line trains provided such journeys on Saturday. Trains of this type had been replaced by new C stock on both the Circle and Hammersmith & City Lines' daily services some months previously.

TERMINALS

London's main-line terminals are, of course, well known. However, there are also many more terminal stations on the various former British Railways and London Transport railway lines in and around London. In this section, we take a look at some of them forty or so years ago.

A long-vanished London terminus is Palace Gates on the former Great Eastern branch from Seven Sisters, intended to serve Alexandra Palace from the east. It was closed along with the branch in January 1963, but for a time the tracks and platforms remained as a shunting neck attached to the nearby Bounds Green carriage depot on the Great Northern main line. This view looks south on 15 August 1974, shortly before all was obliterated by housing development.

This view of Palace Gates station looking north on the same occasion shows how all of its platform buildings have long been demolished. In the distance may be seen the buildings of Bounds Green carriage sheds, which interestingly were provided for the L.N.E.R. by the L.P.T.B. to compensate for the loss of their sheds at Park Junction, Highgate which had been taken over for the extension of the Northern Line over the L.N.E.R. branches from Finsbury Park to Highgate, Alexandra Palace, East Finchley, High Barnet and Edgware in 1939. The G.E.R. branch had not been connected to the G.N.R. here originally, but a link was built by the L.N.E.R. during World War Two connecting it to the former G.N.R. Hertford Loop to provide alternative routeings for troop and goods trains from the north to London's docks in the event of the East Coast main line being disrupted by enemy action. This link too may be seen in the distance, now used only to shunt wagons into the disused station.

Following the end of British Railways steam services in August 1968, only the preserved LNER Pacific No 4472 *Flying Scotsman* was permitted to haul passenger trains over BR metals. Here, on 29 March 1969, it has returned to its spiritual home, Kings Cross station to operate what could have been its last railtour on BR, as it was then due to travel to the USA. Crowds of enthusiasts thronged the terminus on this damp Saturday morning, some even trespassing on the track beyond Platform 1. This photograph was taken from the platform of Kings Cross (York Road) station which was served by up trains on the Great Northern suburban City Widened Lines service, whose track is on the extreme left leading into the tunnel. Much has changed at Kings Cross since. This station and platform are no more, the tunnel is disused and the splendid Great Northern signal box to the right, which controlled movements in and out of the station, has also gone. However, an addition platform – curiously known as 'Platform 0' – has been provided in recent years to the left of Platform 1 where the access road for parcels traffic had been.

LEFT: As previously mentioned, Waterloo was the last London main-line terminus to see steam operation. Here on 15 March 1967, BR Standard class 4MT 4-6-0, No 75068 backs down to couple up to a newspaper train. On the left, a Brush Type 4 diesel then on loan from the Western Region to haul Bournemouth and Weymouth expresses waits alongside pre-war Southern Railway 2HAL and 2BIL EMUs in the sidings beyond Platform 21. The 1950s office blocks along York Road are in the background.

Watford Metropolitan Line terminus has a curious history in that it is situated some distance away from the town centre, adjacent to Cassiobury Park. That was not the intention, however, as when this new branch was built in the early 1920s, the Metropolitan Railway actually built the booking hall and street-level buildings for its intended purpose in Watford Market Place. However, obstinate land owners between this and the eventual terminus refused to sell, so the building became a shop instead. It then became *The Moon Under Water* public house in the early 1990s. Meanwhile, this unusual view taken in July 1969 shows one of the ex-BR Western Region Swindon-built 5700 class 0-6-0PTs purchased by London Transport in the late 1950s. Now numbered L90, it is taking-on water at Watford Metropolitan station as a train of Metropolitan Line A Stock awaits departure for central London. These 0-6-0 PTs hauled rubbish trains containing station or engineering waste to be dumped at nearby Watford tip sidings until they were withdrawn in June 1971. As this book is being compiled, work is finally due to start on linking the Watford branch of the Metropolitan to the former London Midland Region Croxley branch. This will see Metropolitan trains diverted via Watford High Street (on the London Overground Euston to Watford branch) to terminate at Watford Junction. They will finally serve Watford town centre almost 100 years after they were originally meant to!

In August 1969, experimentally rebuilt 1938 tube stock driving motor car 10306 awaits departure with a train to Kennington via Golders Green and Charing Cross at the original Edgware terminus of the Edgware, Highgate & Morden Line, by now called the Northern Line. In the foreground is the third platform added in the 1950s. Beyond it, an additional island platform was built for the abortive extension to Bushey Heath.

During the years this book covers, the East London Line of the London Underground had two southern terminals: New Cross and New Cross Gate. Both provided interchange with BR Southern Region services, on the Central and Eastern sections respectively. Only at New Cross Gate was the East London Line's terminal platform connected directly to the BR network, though this link was later severed. Here on 7 August 1969, a four-car set of Q stock, with a Q27 driving motor leading and a Q38 at the trailing end, arrives at New Cross Gate. Note how the indictors read 'New + Gate, Metropolitan'. At this time, the East London Line was also part of the Metropolitan Line network, despite the fact that the trains were supplied and maintained by the District Line. Also of note is the BR Mk1 locomotive-hauled carriage on the sidings to the east of the East London Line platform, since at this period, this stock did not usually run into London Bridge, Charing Cross or Cannon Street stations. These sidings were later removed and housing development built in their place. Conversely, however, a large depot for the London Overground services which took over the East London Line in 2010 now occupies the space between its V-shaped junction with the Southern main line. These services of course have seen through running restored south of New Cross Gate to Crystal Palace and West Croydon.

Of all the London main-line terminals, Paddington is unique in having Underground trains serving surface platforms adjacent to those in the main line terminal. This results from the original Metropolitan Railway being linked here for through running with the GWR. Here in September 1969, a train of CO stock departs from Paddington for Hammersmith. Note that the destination plate shows 'Metropolitan': the Hammersmith & City Line was a subsidiary of this line at the time.

As mentioned earlier, under the 1935-1940 New Works Programme, the former GNR/LNER branch from Finchley Central (Church End) to Edgware was to have been incorporated within the extended Northern Line and also doubled. At Edgware, it was to be linked with the existing branch from Golders Green and diverted into that line's terminus, as well as being linked with the new extension to Bushey Heath. Although most of the doubling of tracks was completed and much preparatory work at Edgware done, it was abandoned after the war. Photographed on 8 November 1969, Mill Hill East station became the terminus of the branch from Finchley Central when electric services got that far along the line in May 1941. The original Great Northern station buildings remain virtually unaltered, complete with wooden platform. Apart from the latter, the station remains so today. Note the space for the second track – installed but lifted again during the war to replace bomb-damaged tracks elsewhere – on the left.

For many years, steam and then diesel locomotives were stabled between turns at Kings Cross on the locomotive bank to the west side of the terminus. Here on 27 October 1972, Brush Type 4 1999, the 500th of the type to be delivered and in its original BR two-tone green livery, accompanies an English Electric Type 4 and a 'Peak', which are both in BR blue livery. This view was taken looking across the Great Northern suburban tracks from what was then Platform 10, at the western side of the main line part of the station, which for many years was a 'Mecca' for railway enthusiasts.

A group of young train-spotters look on as a *Western Pullman* set led by driving motor W60098 leaves Paddington on 17 April 1973, sending a plume of exhaust fumes into the air as it passes beneath Bishop's Bridge Road. This photograph was taken from Platforms 8 and 9, which for many years were also thronged with railway enthusiasts.

On the approaches to Paddington that same evening, one of the Western Region's 'doomed' Hymek Type 4 (7044) diesel hydraulics passes Paddington's parcel depot on its way to collect empty stock from the main line station. In the background is an early Brush Type 2 (5539), which had been transferred from the Great Eastern to the Western Region to replace such types.

Showing to good effect Brunel's splendid roof at Paddington Station, a *Western Pullman* set awaits departure for Bristol on the evening of 27 April 1973. This particular set, with driving motor car W60092 leading, had originally been one of the *Midland Pullman* units used on the St. Pancras to Manchester Central service from 1960 until the spring of 1966. This service was withdrawn following the inauguration of electric main line services between Euston and Manchester. On the adjacent track 1554, a Brush Type 4, was one of those used to replace the Western Region's diesel hydraulics until Inter City 125 units took over later in the 1970s.

In complete contrast to busy Paddington, this view shows Ongar station on 2 June 1973. This former Great Eastern branch was taken over by the London Underground's Central Line as part of the 1935-1940 New Works Programme, but not electrified until November 1957. Expected urban development resulting from the town being 'on the tube' was thwarted by 'Green Belt' restrictions on further building in the countryside around London after the war. The section of the Central Line beyond Epping to Ongar remained as a single-track branch until closure in 1994. Ongar was the most remote station on London Underground's network.

Driving motor car 11109 heads a seven-car formation of 1938 tube stock at the Drayton Park terminus of the Northern City Line on 20 April 1975. As remarked upon earlier, this station became the northern terminus for the line in 1964 after plans to link it to the surface and extend it to Highgate, Alexandra Palace, East Finchley and High Barnet were abandoned, and its sub-surface terminus at Finsbury Park taken over to provide cross-platform interchange between the Piccadilly Line and the new Victoria Line.

The City Widened Lines and Circle/Metropolitan Line platforms at Moorgate before they were 'entombed' beneath new office developments. In the evening rush hour, on 25 April 1975, Brush Type 2 (31189) and a set of Cravens two-car DMUs with driving motor car E51289 leading are both working the Great Northern inner suburban services to which they were delivered new in 1959/60. Both types and the services will be replaced by the new Great Northern electrics just over eighteen months later.

Cockfosters station, the northern terminus of the Piccadilly Line, typifies the futuristic design of Underground stations in the 1930s. It has a three-platform layout, and is very similar to the re-sited Uxbridge station built at the same time when the Piccadilly Line was extended to the town. This view on 8 May 1975 shows a train of 1959 tube stock, with driving motor car 1195 trailing, ready to depart for Rayners Lane. New 1973 tube stock trains would shortly begin to replace this stock, which was then transferred to the Northern Line to replace earlier 1938 tube stock.

Another obscure London Underground terminus was Shoreditch, on the East London Line. Despite being only a short distance outside the City, it only opened during Monday to Friday rush hours, and on Sunday mornings for the nearby markets. Here 1938 tube stock driving motor car 10186 leads a four-car unit into the terminus on 9 May 1975. Originally, the line was linked to the adjacent Great Eastern main line, with trains running into Liverpool Street, but by the time this was taken, the second platform had long been disused, and the track removed. The station finally closed in June 2006, eventually being replaced by the new Shoreditch High Street station on the link between the former East London and North London Lines on the new London Overground network in April 2010.

Some five weeks before the Northern City Line was closed for the alterations required to accommodate the new British Rail Great Northern electric services, driving motor car 11117 heads a seven-car train of 1938 stock at Moorgate on 29 August 1975. It stands at Platform 9, where six months earlier a train of the same stock over-ran the buffer stops and crashed into the blind tunnel wall. The station clock here shows 7.20pm, and as by now services on this line finished early, this is one of the last trains of the evening.

NORTHERN LINE

The Northern Line on the London Underground is one of the most complicated on the system, and would have been even more so if the extensions planned under the 1935-1940 New Works Programme had been completed. Here we take a look at the line as it was forty to forty-five years ago.

London Transport's 1938 tube stock were synonymous with the Northern Line for forty years. Towards the end of their reign, a seven-car formation of this stock heads north from Burnt Oak towards Edgware on the branch from Golders Green on 15 April 1974.

At the Edgware terminus of the Northern Line, in August 1969, experimental 1938 tube stock driving motor car 10306 awaits departure for Kennington via Charing Cross. In all probability it will traverse the Kennington loop where it terminates, so this car will be facing north when it returns. As we saw earlier, had all of the Northern Line's planned extensions been completed, the line would have continued north of Edgware to Bushey Heath on an alignment originally intended to reach Watford. Today, it is proposed that Northern Line trains which run via Charing Cross to Kennington will be extended on a new line, via a tunnel, to new developments around Battersea power station.

Morden is the southern terminus of the Northern Line, and trains continue some distance south of the station to reach their depot. Here on 19 April 1973, driving motor car 10238 leads a seven-car train of 1938 tube stock out of the depot to take up service. At one time, there were plans to extend the Northern Line to Sutton, but in the event, the Southern Railway built a new branch from Wimbledon to Sutton along a similar alignment, and this has a station at Morden Park behind the Northern Line depot.

LEFT: On the same day that the previous photograph was taken, another train of 1938 tube stock, with which the Northern Line was solely equipped at the time, arrives at Mill Hill East. This station was originally on the Great Northern branch to Edgware from Church End (renamed Finchley Central when taken over by the Northern Line in 1940). By 1941, only the section to Mill Hill East was electrified, due to a nearby military barracks and the requirement for the troops to have easy access. Despite being doubled throughout and also equipped with conductor rails, the complete branch was never electrified, as intended, and the second track was removed during the war to replace bomb damaged rails elsewhere. Ironically, the extension was not formally abandoned until 1964, when part of the track bed was needed for a new slip-road to the M1 motorway. The space where the second track had been is evident on the right.

At one of the Northern Line's other extremities, its High Barnet terminus, driving motor car 10190 heads another seven-car train of 1938 tube stock bound for the Kennington loop via Charing Cross on 31 March 1975. The complicated double junction at Camden Town links the Edgware and High Barnet/Mill Hill East sections of the Northern Line with its inner London Bank and Charing Cross branches, which in turn meet again at Kennington allowing trains from each to continue to Morden. The branch to High Barnet was taken over from the London & North Eastern Railway in 1940 with tube trains from Morden and central London coming to the surface at East Finchley and then over the former Great Northern and LNER branch. However as we will see in more detail later, electrification of the whole branch, south of Highgate to Finsbury Park where it was to link with the Northern City Line, was never completed. There were also plans to extend the branch further north, to the centre of Barnet, as well as to partially rebuild High Barnet station, which remains in virtually original condition today. In the background, a train of 1972 stock is in the sidings to the east of the station.

RIGHT: Except for East Finchley, all the stations on the High Barnet branch of the Northern Line remain in basically original condition. This is seen quite clearly in this view of a train of 1938 tube stock with driving motor car 10282 at its trailing end heading for High Barnet at Woodside Park on 4 April 1975. Former Great Northern stations such as Palmers Green and Winchmore Hill on the Hertford loop are very similar in appearance, although the latter lost its original platform buildings as a result of the 1976 electrification of the branch.

By 31 March 1975, new 1972 tube stock units had been supplied to the Northern Line to supplement the ageing 1938 stock trains which by now were becoming troublesome and were blamed for poor service on the line. The new trains were basically the same as the 1967 stock units on the Victoria Line, but modified for crew operation. Here we see one of the Mk1 type with driving motor car 3528 at its trailing end, departing from Brent station for Edgware. Apart from a few cars transferred to the Victoria and Bakerloo Lines in later years, all of the 1972 Mk1 units remained on the Northern Line. All had been withdrawn before the last 1959 tube stock cars (which had replaced 1938 stock between 1975 and 1978) had been retired in January 2000. On the other hand, virtually all 1972 Mk 2 tube stock cars remain in service today on the Bakerloo Line, where they will remain at least well into the 2020s.

Somewhat oddly, two quaint old Great Northern signal boxes survive to the north of Woodside Park station: one originally controlled a level crossing where Woodside Park Road crossed the tracks, the other the station goods yard on the right, now long converted into a car park. In this view a train of 1938 stock (with driving motor car 11107 trailing) heads for High Barnet on 8 May 1975.

West Finchley station is even quainter. Although looking like a Victorian structure it was not opened until 1932, just eight years before it was taken over by the Northern Line. It was built using materials from stations closed on rural LNER branch lines. Here driving motor car 10297 arrives there with a train of 1938 tube stock, bound for Kennington via Charing Cross on 8 May 1975.

Finchley Central station (originally Church End) is the junction between what had originally been the 'main' line on the Edgware, Highgate & London Railway between Kings Cross, Finsbury Park, Highgate and Edgware and its subsidiary branch to High Barnet. Taken over by the Great Northern and then the London & North Eastern Railway, it was due to be rebuilt under the 1935-1940 New Works Programme with new buildings on the Ballards Lane bridge at the country end of the station. But this was never done and the station is still in original condition. A train of 1938 tube stock departs for Morden via Bank, as another arrives bound for High Barnet on 8 May 1975.

In contrast to the High Barnet branch, stations on the Edgware branch were newly built when what had been the Hampstead tube was extended north of Golders Green in 1923/24. Here, on 8 May 1975, a train of 1938 tube stock departs for Edgware from Burnt Oak station, as a train of 1972 Mk 1 stock train heading into central London arrives.

The isolated Northern City Line, from Moorgate to Drayton Park, was also part of the Northern Line, with which it should have been linked in 1940. Here, on 4 October 1975, a seven-car train of 1938 tube stock stands at Drayton Park terminus: the last day it would be part of the London Underground. The four-road car depot which provided trains for the line is on the right. For the last five years of tube operation, trains were supplied from Bakerloo Line stock kept at Neasden depot, which involved their being towed to the surface at Drayton Park using the southbound ramp built in 1939, to connect the line with the Great Northern main line at Finsbury Park, then south to Kings Cross and down onto the City Widened Lines, and then along the Metropolitan Line to and from Neasden.

SHEDS
AND DEPOTS

For obvious reasons, there have always been several operating sites for the railways in and around London. Traditionally, those housing steam locomotives were colloquially known as 'engine sheds', though technically referred to by British Railways as 'motive power depots', whilst premises housing diesel and electric rolling stock have always been referred to as depots. We see below a number of these establishments as they were in the late 1960s and the 1970s.

A general view of Neasden depot from the south on 18 April 1970 shows trains of Metropolitan Line A stock and Bakerloo Line 1938 tube stock, as well as one of the Underground's battery locomotives. This depot was unusual in housing both sub-surface and tube stock, as it still is today servicing the Jubilee and Metropolitan Lines.

Nine Elms was the last of the many large engine sheds in London that provided locomotives for passenger express work. Here, BR Standard class 5MT 4-6-0 No 73093 is in front of a rebuilt Bulleid Pacific at the coaling stage on 18 March 1967. To the right are heaps of ashes from dropped fires. The air of dilapidation and neglect is not helped by the fact that this large establishment had often attracted the attentions of the *Luftwaffe* during the war, and much of the resulting bomb damage was never fully repaired. Nine Elms closed in July 1967.

Ironically, London Transport was the last state-owned public transport operator to retain standard-gauge steam locomotives. Their own examples in passenger service had been withdrawn in the 1930s, and steam haulage using British Railways locomotives on Metropolitan Line trains between Aylesbury and Rickmansworth, and also on the Chesham shuttle, ended in 1961. However, a number of steam locomotives were retained by London Transport for haulage of goods or engineers' trains on sub-surface sections of the Underground until June 1971. Latterly, these were ex-GWR 5700 class 0-6-0 pannier tank locomotives acquired from the Western Region in the late 1950s. This view taken on 10 June 1968 from the window of a Metropolitan Line train shows their small depot, and coaling and watering plant, at the northern end of London Transport's Neasden depot. Two pannier tanks are visible.

When diesels took over most main line and outer suburban workings from Kings Cross, Broad Street and Moorgate on the Great Northern, a new depot was opened at Finsbury Park in April 1960. It was British Railways' first purpose-built depot dedicated to servicing main-line diesels. Here English Electric Type 2 'Baby Deltic' D5900, the first of the ten delivered for these services in 1959, is out of service and stored in the sidings on 4 May 1969. As mentioned earlier, these locomotives were always troublesome, and less than ten years after they had entered service most had been withdrawn.

Things are not what they appear in this photograph taken on 2 July 1969. The train of 1938 tube stock is not in service on an Underground line, despite the LT-style cable-runs in the foreground. It is on what should have been the south-bound track from Alexandra Palace and Highgate on the Northern City Line north of Finsbury Park station, and is on one of the sections of the Northern Line extensions abandoned after the war. On the right are the carriage sidings in which Great Northern suburban DMUs were stabled, with both Cravens and BR Derby types evident, along with a rake of locomotive-hauled stock. The sidings were situated on the east (up) side of the main line, between it and the tracks meant to have been used for the Northern Line. These too were closed as a result of the Great Northern suburban electrification, for which the former steam shed at Hornsey was adapted as a depot.

This view, taken looking south from West Cromwell Road on 12 July 1969, shows London Transport's Lillie Bridge depot. This had been originally built for the Great Northern, Brompton & Piccadilly Railway (later the Piccadilly Line) and opened in 1906, but after that line was extended in 1932 and provided with new facilities at Cockfosters and Northfields, it became a base for the Underground's fleet of service locomotives. Two battery locomotives are outside the depot: the building to the right housed steam locomotives. A train of District Line R Stock exits the tunnel under the lines as it approaches West Kensington station.

In 1969, Neasden depot also housed a number of the Underground's service locomotives. Here on 5 August 1969, battery locomotive L22, one of the 1964/65 Metro-Cammell/GEC batch, is coupled to old Standard Stock trailers used to carry workmen on engineers' trains around the network. The locomotives had two sets of couplings, compatible to tube or sub-surface rolling stock.

Two (L89 and L94) of the ex-GWR class 5700 pannier tanks, used by London Transport for stores and engineers' trains, stand outside their shed at Lillie Bridge depot on 16 August 1969. The number '510' on the smokebox door of the left-hand locomotive is not its stock number, but the duty number of the train it had been operating. These were the last steam locomotives allocated to the District Line, and despite not having condensing apparatus, they sometimes worked through the tunnels of the Circle Line.

At Lillie Bridge depot on the same day, are two old Standard (pre-1938) tube stock motor cars which have been retained for shunting work on electrified tracks in depots, as well as hauling stores or ballast trains over the system when the current is on. At this time, all London Transport's service locomotives, including the steam, were painted in a maroon livery similar to that used on Metropolitan Railway electric locomotives. This was changed to yellow in the early 1980s.

Contrasting sharply with the more modern, flared-sided R stock cars on the left, an elderly Q23 driving motor car heads a train of District Line Q stock in Ealing Common depot on 18 October 1970. This depot, originally built for the District Railway, was supplemented in 1959 by a new depot at Upminster, the eastern end of the line.

The small depot at Drayton Park that serviced the Northern City Line photographed on 20 April 1975. Two trains of 1938 tube stock are on shed, with driving motor car 10115 nearest the camera. The structure to the right of the shed is the electric supply substation built to provide power for the Great Northern & City Line, and is still in use today. Located between the northbound running track and the former LNER Ashburton Grove sidings, which served Islington Council's main rubbish dump, the depot was demolished after the line was taken over by British Rail's Great Northern electrics in 1976. Today, the site is overgrown, which is a disgrace when it could provide adequate space for additional platform capacity for the Emirates Stadium (home of Arsenal Football Club). The little Drayton Park station – which is closed on match days, forces spectators to walk to and from either Highbury & Islington Arsenal or Finsbury Park stations.

FINBSURY PARK

Finsbury Park was once an important junction on the suburban lines of the Great Northern and, later, the London & North Eastern Railway, with the lines to Highgate, Alexandra Palace, High Barnet and Edgware diverging to the north of the station, and those to Canonbury Tunnel, Broad Street and the docks to its south. Today, the only passenger services that diverge there from the main line are those which took over the Northern City Line to Moorgate in 1976. Here we see Finsbury Park in the diesel years.

In addition to being an important junction and interchange station on the Great Northern main line, Finsbury Park also was the location of British Railways' first purpose-built depot meant for main line passenger diesel locomotives. This view on 6 May 1969 shows four of the ten ill-fated English Electric 'baby Deltics' out of use at the depot.

One of London Transport's 1964/65 Metro-Cammell/GEC battery locomotives (L21), hauling 1938 tube stock from Highgate depot to Drayton Park on the isolated Northern City Line in June 1969. It is just about to cross the East Coast main line north of Finsbury Park station. The signal box on the right is Finsbury Park No.7, which by this time was manned only once a week to supervise the movement of Underground rolling stock between Drayton Park and Highgate.

The same train has now reached Finsbury Park station, and is passing through Platform 1 on its way to Drayton Park. On the right, are the half-finished extra platforms for the line that 1938 tube stock trains should have used from Moorgate to Highgate, Alexandra Palace, East Finchley and High Barnet.

For more than thirty years, the rusting skeleton of the uncompleted new station façade and additional high-level platforms for the Northern City Line at Finsbury Park station remained an eyesore. A view taken from the 'temporary' booking hall, on a dismal 23 November 1969, shows the 'stairway to nowhere' that would have served the island platform for both northbound and southbound Underground trains. Station Place at Finsbury Park had to be moved eastwards to accommodate this structure, entailing the demolition of the Victorian buildings that faced the station.

This view, taken on 4 August 1970, from the western boundary of Finsbury Park shows London Transport's battery locomotive L21 climbing towards the Highgate branch with a three-car train of 1938 tube stock returning to Highgate. Such workings ran beneath the main line south of the station, taking up the down track which the last shuttle service trains from Finsbury Park to Highgate and Alexandra Palace had used prior to their withdrawal in July 1954. This track passed above the down slow and down goods line. Finsbury Park carriage sidings are in the left foreground, while a container freight heads south on the up goods, probably bound for the docks via Canonbury Tunnel.

By 14 October 1972, the rusting unfinished station structure at Finsbury Park had finally been demolished, but the wooden fencing and 'temporary' booking office would remain for some time. Station Place is still cobbled, while one of London Transport's DMS-class buses, which had replaced Routemaster buses on route 106 two months previously, is seen on the extreme right.

On the same day as the previous photograph, a Brush Type 4 diesel heads a down express north of Finsbury Park. It passes under the bridge which carried the tracks from the Highgate and Alexandra Palace branch to the up side of the main line, and into the carriage sidings. This bridge would soon be demolished as part of the Great Northern suburban electrification scheme. The photograph was taken from the footbridge which crossed the railway from the park: This was also replaced.

Looking north from the same footbridge, a train of four two-car Cravens DMUs heads for Kings Cross on the up main north of Finsbury Park. The track furthest to the right is a siding leading to the carriage sidings south of the bridge. Carriages stabled here were often targets for vandals who hurled missiles from the football pitch above, and so the siding is no longer there today.

A rare survivor photographed, on 9 September 1973, from the window of a train passing Finsbury Park diesel depot is BR Eastern Region departmental locomotive DB968000 now in use as a static electric train heater. This was one of the BTH Type 1 diesels originally numbered in the D8200 series and allocated to the Eastern Region. A Deltic diesel and a Cravens DMU are just visible on the left. Note also the disused signal gantry, with the 'semaphores' removed.

The demolition of the ramp taking the down track towards Highgate seen from the window of the down *Cambridge Buffet Express* on 10 December 1972. The two tracks on the left are the down goods (left) and down slow (right).

EAST LONDON
LINE

Originally the East London Railway, including Brunel's Thames Tunnel between Wapping and Rotherhithe, had been operated by main line railways with both goods and passenger traffic, but by the time the photographs in this collection were taken it had become a backwater of the London Underground. Usually, some of the oldest rolling stock worked it, passed down from either the District or Metropolitan Lines. We take a look at the line in those days here, all a far cry from the crowded London Overground Class 378 units that traverse the East London Line in the mid-2010s.

I hope readers will forgive this somewhat gloomy picture of an East London Line unit led by a Q23 driving motor car at Whitechapel, taken on 31 January 1971 shortly before the last trains of this type were withdrawn from service.

Q Stock from the District Line worked East London Line services in 1969, despite the fact that the line was a subsidiary of the Metropolitan Line as the indicator of this Q27 stock driving motor car implies. The train is seen arriving at Whitechapel station from Shoreditch in the evening rush hour of 1 July 1969. Its crew appear to be sloppy in operating it, as the train shows no destination – was it going to New Cross or New Cross Gate? Once aboard, passengers would have had no way of knowing, as these elderly units did not have the public address systems and internal digital destination displays we know today.

A Q27 car waiting to depart from Shoreditch station in the evening rush hour on 7 August 1969 correctly shows its destination as 'New + Gate'. This station was open for the rush hours and even then it was lightly used. It was also opened on Sunday mornings for the nearby Club Row and Petticoat Lane markets.

A Q27 driving motor car heads a four-car unit at the New Cross terminus of the East London Line on the evening of 7 August 1969: it is anyone's guess as to whether it is bound for Shoreditch, or for Whitechapel. At this station, unlike New Cross Gate, there was no opportunity for trains to continue south from the East London Line's terminal platform onto the Southern Region, whose trains here run from Cannon Street and Charing Cross towards Lewisham.

At the New Cross Gate terminus on the East London Line. One of the oldest Q23 Stock driving motor cars still in use heads a train bound for Whitechapel, on 6 September 1969, in the capable hands of motorman Richard Evans. The BR Southern Region sidings on the left have been replaced by housing development.

Looking north on the evening of 6 September 1969 at New Cross Gate, a four-car mixed Q stock unit headed by a Q27 driving motor car contrasts with a BR 0-6-0 Class 08 diesel shunter in the Southern Region sidings. Confusingly, the destination board shows 'New Cross', but this display has already been put up for when it returns from Whitechapel on its next southbound journey.

Following the delivery of new C stock trains to the Circle and Hammersmith & City Lines in 1970/71, Q stock was finally withdrawn and replaced by CO/CP stock displaced from those lines. Instead of four-car formations as before, these ran in five-car sets on the East London Line. One of these trains heads south from Surrey Docks station on 13 May 1973. This station was renamed Surrey Quays some ten years later.

An unusual visitor to the East London Line, on 13 May 1973, was a seven-car train of 1938 tube stock which worked the 'Metro-Tube Tour' over much of the sub-surface system of the Underground. Photographed at New Cross Gate, the train was headed by driving motor car 11054.

When the above tour took place, operation of tube stock on the East London Line would have seemed fanciful. However, trains of the same 1938 tube stock took over services in May 1975, and remained there until January 1977. The recently overhauled driving motor car 11084 heads a train at New Cross terminus on 28 March 1975. Once again, the destination board is set for the return journey from Whitechapel to New Cross Gate.

Driving motor 11106 arriving at Whitechapel from Shoreditch bound for New Cross on 9 May 1975. This photograph clearly shows how much lower the floor of these tube trains was from platform level on the East London Line. This is something that would never be permitted in today's 'Health & Safety' climate.

The floor to platform height difference is very obvious in this view at Shoreditch terminus. Driving motor car 11186 and this four-car train of 1938 tube stock looks quite out of place. From January 1977, four-car units of A Stock from the Metropolitan Line were used on the East London Line, and apart from a short period in the early 1980s when new District Line D stock was used, they remained there until the end of 2007.

NORTHERN
WASTES

Without doubt, the greatest blot on the history of the London Underground is the abandonment of the uncompleted extensions to the Northern Line. These had to be placed in abeyance during the Second World War, and despite London Transport's intention to complete them as soon as possible after hostilities ended, even to the point of quoting intended opening dates on publicly-issued Underground maps (as had also happened before the war), they were abandoned in the early 1950s. The extensions on the Central Line had similarly been put on hold during the war, yet they were completed taking tube trains out into the countryside of south-west Essex. Yet the imposition of the Green Belt around London was used as the excuse to abandon the uncompleted Northern Line extensions. This was patently ridiculous when applied to the section of line between Drayton Park, Finsbury Park, Highgate and Alexandra Palace as this was in an area that had been fully built up during Victorian times, while the section between Mill Hill East and Edgware had also been largely fully developed

between the two world wars. Both of these lines were parts of the existing ex-Great Northern and LNER branches that had already been linked to, and included in, the Northern Line, i.e. from East Finchley to High Barnet and Mill Hill East. Even the new extension north of Edgware toward Bushey Heath could have been justified on the grounds that it was needed to access the major new Northern Line depot being built at Aldenham. But all was abandoned, despite some £3,000,000 having been spent on them and the fact that the two former LNER branches even had conductor rails and fittings for power and signal cabling installed, also electricity substations built. The work included the surface-level station at Highgate which was completely rebuilt, providing direct interchange with the new tube station below. Even the destination plates were made for the new 1938 tube stock trains meant to operate these lines, as were many of the station signs and line describers. Here we see what the remnants of this scheme looked line in the late 1960s and early 1970s.

Although goods traffic on the uncompleted parts of the Northern Line extensions ceased in 1964, the section between Highgate and Drayton Park was used solely for the exchange of tube stock between those points to and from the isolated Northern City Line until the autumn of 1970. Here on 6 May 1969, London Transport battery locomotive L21 hauls a unit of 1938 tube stock southbound out of Highgate East tunnel on tracks this stock should have used in service some thirty years earlier.

This illustrates how near to completion the electrification of the line from Finsbury Park to Highgate was when work stopped in 1940: the large building to the right of the down line at Crouch Hill is a substation for supplying current to the line. Contrary to what has been published elsewhere in recent years, this building was also fully equipped. Cabling was installed throughout at the lineside, and conductor rails fitted to most of the track. All of this equipment was removed before the British Railways steam-operated shuttle service, using gas-lit Victorian rolling stock, was finally withdrawn in July 1954.

Taken the same day as the previous photograph: the view from the entrance to Highgate East Tunnel looking south along the down track. This twin-bore tunnel, (and that to the west of Highgate Station), is typical of the part-elliptical shape used by the Great Northern Railway as also seen on the main line between Finsbury Park and Stevenage. Remnants of the cabling for fourth-rail electrification and signalling are visible on the right-hand wall of the tunnel. The footbridge visible, like the tracks, has long-since been removed, but the tunnels remain, with gates to prevent unauthorised entry.

Without doubt the most striking example of the scandalous waste involved in the abandonment of the Northern Line's uncompleted extensions is Highgate High Level station. The existing LNER surface-level station, in the cutting below Archway Road between the two tunnels, was completely rebuilt in the typical style of Underground architecture of the period as shown here, with direct links to the new tube station on the Northern Line's new tunnel extension from Archway to East Finchley below it. The sloping structure on the left is the shaft for the steep escalator from the station to Archway Road.

At first sight, this looks exactly as a tube train would have done heading towards Finsbury Park from Highgate if the extension had been completed and opened for Northern City Line trains running from Moorgate to Highgate and Alexandra Palace or East Finchley (with rush hour extensions to High Barnet). Sadly, however, it is actually being towed by a battery locomotive (again L21, which for some reason was always used for such moves at this time) and is on the weekly transfer of 1938 tube stock units from Highgate to Drayton Park, seen on 2 July 1969 crossing above the East Coast main line to the east side of Finsbury Park station.

On the same occasion, the 'cortege' awaits its path through Finsbury Park Station and Highbury Vale sidings to Drayton Park. 1938 tube stock driving motor car 11252 is at the rear of the four-car unit. In the foreground may be seen more of the cabling supports installed for the abortive electrification.

The very dilapidated booking office for the branch terminus at Alexandra Palace photographed 8 November 1969. By now, the platforms had long been removed and the site used for car auctions. The British Railways Board Research Department Laboratories were in fact built across the track alignment to the south of the station. Ironically, the station booking office survived the disastrous fire that destroyed much of Alexandra Palace (for a second time) in July 1980 and has since been carefully restored to accommodate a community centre. The former laboratory has become a gymnasium.

Taken on the same day, little remains of Cranley Gardens station. Tracks were lifted in the late 1950s, and then the wooden platform buildings and booking office were burnt out by vandals. Sheltered homes for the elderly were built on this site in the early 1970s, but the bridge seen in the background carrying Muswell Hill Road above the trackbed remains. The line's path around to the site of Muswell Hill station over the St. James Lane viaduct today forms part of Haringey Council's Parkland Walk, which allows people to have scenic views across London.

At Edgware station on 23 November 1969, the overgrown remains of the island platform, built to serve through trains to and from Bushey Heath, are visible on the left. The recently built footbridge from the booking hall to the three platforms that are in use has obstructed the path of the southbound track from Bushey Heath. The works on the new extension north of Edgware were begun only a few weeks before the outbreak of the Second World War, and abandoned in the early 1950s.

Abandonment of the section of existing railway between Mill Hill East and Edgware was just as absurd as that of the Finsbury Park to Highgate link. Ironically, the line from Finchley Central (Church End) to Edgware was scheduled to be closed temporarily from 10 September 1939 – a week after the outbreak of war – to enable the branch to be doubled and electrified. The second track was installed throughout, along with conductor rails, and near Page Street, Mill Hill, a substation (left) was also built but this one was not fully equipped.

To the northwest of the previous picture, Mill Hill (The Hale) was a halt approximately half-way between Mill Hill East and Edgware. It was situated adjacent to the Midland main line's Mill Hill Broadway station, with the branch track passing beneath it. Under the Northern Line's extension plans, the halt would have become a major interchange with the main line, and here we see the concrete extension to the original wooden single platform beneath Bunns Lane. This would have been the southbound (up) platform; and an entirely new northbound (down) platform was built too. By the time this was taken, it had disappeared under spoil from the construction of the nearby M1 Motorway.

The Finsbury Park to Highgate branch: the platform buildings at Crouch End station were removed early in 1967, but the Great Northern-style booking office on Crouch End Hill survived until 1978. Here, London Transport battery locomotive L21, is hauling a three-car unit of 1938 tube stock towards Drayton Park on 2 July 1969. It is noticeable how the platforms had been rebuilt to a 'compromise' height, i.e. to accommodate both full-size main line rolling stock and tube stock, and also have typical Underground-style ridged edging (to assist blind people). Otherwise, Crouch End station would have remained in original condition, like those on the High Barnet branch. By this time, stock transfer trains could only use the southbound (up) track, since the down was obstructed by a heavy wooden strut (visible under the booking office) used to support the weak bridge.

One of the most bizarre sights ever seen on the Finsbury Park to Highgate branch was London Transport's track-testing train, composed of two 1960 tube stock driving motor cars and two Standard (pre-1938) tube stock trailers, which was towed to and from the Northern City Line, in order to test the track. Here on 1 July 1970, it is returning to Highgate through the disused Crouch End station. As far as I am aware, a friend with me that day and were the only people to photograph this train traversing the branch, all thanks to being 'tipped the wink' about its operation by a friend working at London Transport's headquarters: some LT officials aboard the test train were not amused when they saw us.

Photographed on 1 December 1973 from the car park of *The Woodman* public house built above the portals of Highgate West Tunnel, the modern buildings of High Level station sit amid the now trackless path of the Finsbury Park to Highgate branch. In the distance are the entrances to the High East Tunnel: it is easy to imagine this location to be haunted, as many locals believe. Just visible on the left, is the original Great Northern Railway stationmaster's house and it is still there today, overshadowed by the disused platform buildings.

LEFT: A wintry scene on 26 December 1970, looking south towards Stroud Green and Finsbury Park from the footbridge just south of Crouch End station. The substation on the right adjacent to the bridge carrying Crouch Hill over the railway was subsequently adapted as a sports hall for Islington Council's nearby Crouch Hill community centre. Two months or so before this was taken, stock transfers along this route ceased, and the tracks were lifted during 1971. Today, the path of the railway between Finsbury Park and Highgate, is used for Haringey Council's so-called Parkland Walk, and remains completely unobstructed even to the point that bridges along it have been rebuilt with adequate clearance for at least a single-track railway – so is it too much to hope that the branch could yet be reinstated?

ONGAR OUTPOST

While the Northern Line extensions in inner North London, which were put 'on hold' as a result of the war, were abandoned in the early 1950s, with 'Green Belt' around London being used as the most unlikely justification for doing so, the Central Line's extensions out to Epping and, deep into the heart of rural Essex at Ongar – well beyond the Green Belt – were completed, despite also being placed in abeyance during the war. Electrification of the Ongar branch – as late as November 1957 – was patently absurd when the branches between Finsbury Park, Highgate and Alexandra Palace, and between Mill Hill East and Edgware, had been abandoned, especially when much of the materials installed was salvaged and used to electrify this quiet country branch. Moreover, had the Epping to Ongar branch been part of the British Railways network when the notorious Dr Beeching wielded his 'axe' in the early 1960s, it would undoubtedly have been closed. Perhaps the sections of the Central Line's eastern extensions between Hainault and Woodford and even north of Loughton or Debden would have met with the same fate. When the photographs of the Epping to Ongar branch in this section were taken, closure was indeed threatened by London Transport, but did not actually take place until the end of September 1994. Today, the Epping Ongar Railway is a successful heritage line working a variety of steam and diesel rolling stock over most of the line.

Although the Central Line shuttle service between Epping and Ongar was usually worked with just one four-car unit of 1962 tube stock at this time on a single-track, a passing loop and additional platform had been provided at North Weald to allow a second train to run there to and from Epping in rush hours. In the evening rush hour of 28 September 1970, therefore, two units are seen together at North Weald, whose original platform is on the right.

By 7 August 1969 when this was taken, four-car sets of Central Line 1962 tube stock worked the Epping to Ongar shuttle service. Here, driving motor car 1504 heads a train awaiting departure for Ongar from Epping station's platform two. At this period, the shuttle service usually used this platform, whilst the through service to central London and beyond used the other one. Today, both platforms are used by these latter.

Blake Hall station, one of two intermediate stations on the Epping to Ongar section (the other was North Weald) was the quietest station on the London Underground for very many years. It was situated well away from the village, among farmland and rolling countryside. I took this photograph on 7 August 1969, from the door of a 1962 tube stock train. The gentleman who has just walked from the booking office to the platform, probably the station foreman, looks either startled thinking a stranger is going to alight there, or perhaps annoyed since taking photographs on Underground stations was frowned upon by London Transport at the time. This station was closed at the end of October 1981, after which it became a private residence.

My train has now arrived at the Ongar terminus, which was just a single platform, albeit with space for a second track on the right. Standard London Transport Underground signage may be seen at the top left of this picture. In the line's early days, there had been suggestions of extending it to Chelmsford, which the alignment faced and which was not too far away, to provide a relief route from the existing Great Eastern main line to Ipswich and Norwich, but it was not to be.

A view from the footbridge at Epping station. Central Line 1962 tube stock driving motor car 1503 arrives, on 1 June 1977, with the four-car shuttle train from Ongar. Interestingly, this is at the other end of the same unit that I saw nearly eight years earlier on the same service. In the foreground, another 1962 stock train awaits departure for central London and the west. At the time of writing, trains on the Epping Ongar heritage railway cannot reach Epping owing to the lack of suitable terminal facilities, so a vintage bus link to North Weald station has to be provided. The final solution to this problem would seem to be to provide a new terminal platform east of the bridge, with a walkway connection to the Underground station.

LEFT: The booking office and station house at Ongar, taken on 2 June 1973, shows how it has similar architecture to the other three stations on the branch, and indeed others (for instance Snaresbrook) on the 'main' Central Line's eastern extensions over former Great Eastern Railway tracks. Also there had been extensive goods yards and a small engine shed at Ongar. Most of the land was sold off for housing development after the closure of the line in 1994. This is why the main depot of the Epping Ongar heritage line, for the present, is at North Weald.

This view shows North Weald's station house and booking office, which are little changed today when they form the headquarters of the Epping Ongar heritage railway.

North Weald station was unique on the London underground system at this time in having a level crossing over fourth-rail electrified track, at the eastern end of the station servicing a farm track and footpath. In this view, no fewer than three London Transport signs may be seen instructing on its proper use!

This view of a unit of 1962 tube stock approaching Blake Hall station from Ongar bound for Epping in entirely rural countryside shows what a mockery electrifying this outpost made of abandoning the uncompleted Northern Line extensions! It is of note, however, that space did exist for a second track to be installed.

Long abandoned, the engine shed and goods yard at Ongar station is disappearing under foliage when seen on 26 September 1974. The shed had been an outstation of Stratford, which serviced such as the ex-Great Eastern F5-class 2-4-2T's that worked the branch until its electrification in 1957, whilst the goods yard continued in use until the early 1960's. Sadly, this site had been taken over by housing development by the time today's Epping Ongar heritage railway was established, obliging them to build new facilities at North Weald station.

ACCIDENTS

Fortunately, railway accidents are very rare when compared to those on Britain's roads, and those on the London Underground are even rarer. Here we see the after-effects of some of the latter forty to forty-five or so years ago.

A sad sight at Neasden depot on 18 April 1970 is this 1938 tube stock driving motor car whose cab has been completely crushed. It happened in a shunting accident in which, not surprisingly, the driver was killed.

Accident-damaged rolling stock is often kept away from public view in depots. Here a Bakerloo Line 1938 tube stock driving motor car which had been involved in a fatal shunting accident is hidden behind one of London Transport's ancient 1900-built former Central London Railway driving motor cars converted for use as a sleet locomotive, at Neasden depot on 5 August 1969.

At the District Line Ealing Common depot in June 1972, this former Standard (pre-1938) tube stock driving motor car, latterly used as a depot shunter, is seen after an accident. It has been dumped on sidings at the rear of the depot near to Acton Town station, an area which staff often referred to as 'the Alps', where withdrawn rolling stock was stored. Today, 'withdrawn rolling stock' is also stored at this site in very different circumstances – it is now the so-called 'Acton Depot' of the London Transport Museum, and houses many and more interesting road and railway exhibits than those kept at its main Covent Garden location.

Inside Ealing Common depot, a former Standard stock driving motor car – after the shunting accident with the Standard (pre-1938) tube stock driving motor car (see page 163) – is being cannibalised for spare parts.

The worst peacetime accident on London's Underground occurred during the morning rush hour of Friday 28 February 1975. A seven-car train of 1938 tube stock, packed with commuters, crashed into the blind tunnel wall at the end of Platform 9 at Moorgate station. As a result forty-three people died in the accident the cause of which has never been established. Here, at lunchtime on the day of the accident, London Transport service vehicle 1275LD, a special emergency tender mounted on a Leyland 'Titan' PD3 bus chassis, is seen with two Greater London Council fire appliances outside the Moorfields entrance to the station. Remarkably, the Circle and Metropolitan Lines and even the main Northern Line directly beneath the crash site remained open while rescue and recovery operations were being carried out.

The Northern City's terminus was closed for several days after the accident. Photographed on 12 March 1975, is the vastly enlarged sand drag at the entrance to the blind tunnel; the scene of the crash. The notice board by the tunnel mouth asks for anyone who was on this platform at the time of the crash to contact the Police or the station manager. A train of 1938 tube stock, the same stock as the crash train, has halted close to the stop light.

At Piccadilly Circus on 30 October 1975, another train of 1938 tube stock crashed into the dividing wall between the two tunnels at the northern end of the Bakerloo Line station. Fortunately, it was out of service and reversing from the southbound to the northbound track on the crossover at that point and, apparently, took the crossover at too great a speed, causing the train to divide in the middle. The cab of the leading driving motor car (10146) of the trailing unit slammed into the dividing wall and was completely smashed (see above). The trailing end of the same car also suffered serious impact damage after being struck by the trailer car. Serious damage was caused to track and also the signal cabling, which resulted in the closure of the Bakerloo Line for several days. Interestingly, perhaps since it was only eight months after the Moorgate disaster, this serious accident received virtually no press coverage. I was lucky to get this image: thanks to a friend involved in the recovery operation who smuggled me down to the site. Here, London Transport engineers do their best to extricate the damaged train.

ABOVE & RIGHT: Just over a week later, on 7 November 1975, the wreckage of 10146 has been towed to the Bakerloo Line's London Road, Elephant & Castle depot. The top view looks towards where the driver's cab was from inside the car; the lower view shows just how badly damaged the cab was by the impact. Part of the roof had to be cut away as it was entangled with the mass of cabling on the tunnel walls that the impact dislodged. One of the engineers involved in its recovery stands next to the wreck.

DESIGN CLASSICS

Without doubt, the architectural designs, and that of rolling stock produced for the London Passenger Transport Board (better known as London Transport) in the 1930s were classics, and it is most unfortunate that their evolution came to an abrupt halt as a result of the Second World War. On the London Underground, this was epitomised by the splendid 1938 tube stock and O and P sub-surface stock (later known as CO and CP). Both types were still going strong during the period this book covers.

The longest-lasting of the classic 1930's designs of London underground trains are the 1938 tube stock units, some of which survive to this day in service on the Ilse of Wight. Their use there was all in the future when this view of one of these trains was taken at Harrow-On-The-Hill on 8 June 1969. It is off the beaten track for this type, being a pair of Bakerloo Line units en route from Neasden depot to Acton Works for overhaul, entailing a trip on the Metropolitan Line's Uxbridge branch (to which it is burrowing beneath the northbound Amersham and Aylesbury tracks) as far as Rayners Lane, then reversal and southbound along the Piccadilly Line's Uxbridge branch.

On 1 July 1969, a seven-car train of tube stock, with an earlier Standard stock trailer as its penultimate car, leaves Queens Park station to descend into the Bakerloo Line's original tunnels on its subterranean journey to Elephant & Castle. These units lasted on this line until November 1985, and then after a break of a year or so, some were refurbished and returned to the Northern Line for a further eighteen months: finally being withdrawn in the spring of 1988. Even that was not the end of the story, since many of these survivors were sent to the Isle of Wight, where some remain in service to this day.

The most distinctive-looking Underground rolling stock to appear in the 1930s (other than the short-lived streamlined 1935 tube stock cars) was the O and P sub-surface types, with their flared sides. These were first introduced in 1937 and ran originally on the Circle, Hammersmith & City and Metropolitan Lines, along with similar cars (classified Q38) that operated in mixed formations with older stock on the District Line. Many of these latter cars were modified after the war to run with newer cars of the same general design, becoming R stock on the District Line and some cars of this type were built as late as 1959. Here, on 1 July 1969, a train of CO stock (as O stock became known after modifications) is seen at Bromley-By-Bow, operating what was then the Hammersmith & City Line's rush hour extension to Barking.

Perhaps this distinctive design is most associated with the Circle Line. A unit of CP stock departs from Gloucester Road Station on an 'outer rail' (clockwise) Circle Line service in the evening rush hour on 4 August 1969. O and CO stock worked the Circle Line for most of the 1950s and 1960s, before being displaced by new C69 stock in 1970/71. However, this train of CP stock was new as a P stock unit to the Metropolitan Line, from which it was displaced by new A stock in the early 1960s.

Although 1938 tube stock is most commonly associated with the Bakerloo and Northern Lines, where it replaced Standard (pre-1938) tube stock when new, a few trains of this type also worked on the Piccadilly Line, at first alongside Standard stock, and then 1959 tube stock. Here on 7 August 1969, one of these trains has just come out of the siding at Rayners Lane to take the long journey through Central London to Cockfosters. I have always suspected that these trains should have been allocated when new to the Northern Line, but were not needed when the intended takeover of the lines between Finsbury Park and Alexandra Palace, those between Mill Hill East and Edgware, and the new line onwards to Bushey Heath, was abandoned.

The modern-looking Q38 stock cars at the trailing end of this mixed formation of Q stock seen leaving West Brompton station on a District Line service to Wimbledon, on 7 August 1969. Although in some cases built only two or three years earlier, the older Q stock cars look positively dated in comparison.

A final look at one of these distinctive, flared-sided trains: a CO stock unit working the 'inner rail' Circle Line service at Moorgate station on 12 August 1969. In the background, the Barbican development is finally rising from the ruins left by wartime bombing.

What should have been? Photographed on 2 July 1969, a three-car unit of 1938 tube stock is towed through the closed Crouch End Station on its way from Drayton Park to the Northern Line's Highgate depot. Note the platform edge is at the correct height for the train, having been rebuilt in 1939 in anticipation of the Northern City Line being extended through to Highgate, Alexandra Palace and East Finchley.

A seven-car train of 1938 tube stock arrives at Queensbury station heading for Stanmore on 20 April 1975. The Stanmore branch was opened in 1932 by the Metropolitan Railway, but was taken over by the Bakerloo Line a few weeks after the war broke out in 1939. The station, which had originally been little more than a halt, was substantially rebuilt in typical 1930s style, but still has wooden platforms.

The Northern Line was also equipped with 1938 tube stock, many of the cars originally being owned by the London & North Eastern Railway over whose suburban branches the Northern Line was meant to be extended. But this scheme was never completed. Here a seven-car train of 1938 tube stock enters Finchley Central station from the Mill Hill East branch on 8 May 1975, running on sections of the former LNER branch that were electrified in 1940/41. This station should have been rebuilt with new, Chas. Holden-designed buildings on the bridge, which carries Ballards Lane over the railway. In the event, the original GNR buildings were retained.

Although some cars of 1938 tube stock survive on the Isle of Wight, and others have been preserved by London Underground, the vast majority were scrapped. Many were taken away by road: here in a lucky photograph taken from my office window at Gardiner's Corner, Aldgate on 2 November 1977, half of 1938 tube stock driving motor car 10303, along with one bogie, is carried on a low-loader after being collected from the Morden depot on the Northern Line.

THE
LAST DROP

To end this selection of my railway photographs for the period 1967-1977, we take a final look at the last working state-owned steam locomotives running in the London area.

On 6 June 1971, a special train ran from Moorgate (Met) to Neasden to commemorate the withdrawal of the last steam engines used on the London Underground. Here, ex-Western Region 5700 Class 0-6-0PT L94 is the centre of attention for photographers at Farringdon station as it passes through to pick up its train at Moorgate.

As is well-known, the former London & South Western Railway's main line into Waterloo was the last to operate passenger steam locomotives into the London area. Here, on a damp 7 February 1967, BR Standard class 5MT 4-6-0, No 73115 *King Pellinore* backs out of Waterloo after bringing in a boat train from Southampton Docks. This was one of twenty of this type supplied to the Western section of the Southern Region in 1956/57 to replace thirty-year-old SR King Arthur class 4-6-0s. Sadly, they lasted barely ten years and this was one of the last survivors: 73115 was built in November 1956 and withdrawn at the end of March 1967. The notice on the hut at the end of Platform 11 warns trainspotters were not allowed to congregate at that point. Of course, having reached the 'ripe old age' of 19 at that time, I no longer looked upon myself as such, but as a serious railway enthusiast and photographer. No one took any notice of this warning anyway, including BR staff that ignored the increasing numbers of us who gathered there as the last day of steam approached.

RIGHT: London Transport had the dubious honour of operating the last state-owned standard-gauge steam locomotives, in the whole of the United Kingdom. Here on 8 June 1969, former Western Region 5700 class 0-6-0 pannier tank L90 heads north through Harrow-On-The-Hill station with a rubbish train bound for Watford tip sidings. Refuse from stations as well as old ballast and other waste left over from track renewals was taken there to be dumped in land-fill sites.